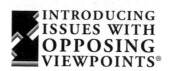

INTRODUCING
ISSUES WITH
OPPOSING
VIEWPOINTS®

Media Bias

Ebonie Ledbetter, *Book Editor*

GREENHAVEN PRESS
A part of Gale, Cengage Learning

GALE
CENGAGE Learning·

Farmington Hills, Mich • San Francisco • New York • Waterville, Maine
Meriden, Conn • Mason, Ohio • Chicago

Patricia Coryell, *Vice President & Publisher, New Products & GVRL*
Douglas Dentino, *Manager, New Products*
Judy Galens, *Acquisitions Editor*

For more information, contact:
Greenhaven Press
27500 Drake Rd.
Farmington Hills, MI 48331-3535
Or you can visit our Internet site at gale.cengage.com

For product information and technology assistance, contact us at

Gale Customer Support, 1-800-877-4253
For permission to use material from this text or product, submit all requests online at
www.cengage.com/permissions

Further permissions questions can be e-mailed to permissionrequest@cengage.com

Articles in Greenhaven Press anthologies are often edited for length to meet page require-ments. In addition, original titles of these works are changed to clearly present the main thesis and to explicitly indicate the author's opinion. Every effort is made to ensure that Greenhaven Press accurately reflects the original intent of the authors. Every effort has been made to trace the owners of copyrighted material.

Cover image © Bloomua/Shutterstock.com

LIBRARY OF CONGRESS CATALOGING-IN-PUBLICATION DATA

Media bias / Ebonie Ledbetter, book editor.
    pages cm. -- (Introducing issues with opposing viewpoints)
  Includes bibliographical references and index.
  ISBN 978-0-7377-7236-4 (hardcover)
  1. Mass media--Objectivity--United States--Juvenile literature. I. Ledbetter, Ebonie, editor
  P96.O242U656 2015
  302.23'0973--dc23
      2014035143

Printed in the United States of America
1 2 3 4 5 6 7 19 18 17 16 15

Contents

Foreword

Indulging in a wide spectrum of ideas, beliefs, and perspectives is a critical cornerstone of democracy. After all, it is often debates over differences of opinion, such as whether to legalize abortion, how to treat prisoners, or when to enact the death penalty, that shape our society and drive it forward. Such diversity of thought is frequently regarded as the hallmark of a healthy and civilized culture. As the Reverend Clifford Schutjer of the First Congregational Church in Mansfield, Ohio, declared in a 2001 sermon, "Surrounding oneself with only like-minded people, restricting what we listen to or read only to what we find agreeable is irresponsible. Refusing to entertain doubts once we make up our minds is a subtle but deadly form of arrogance." With this advice in mind, Introducing Issues with Opposing Viewpoints books aim to open readers' minds to the critically divergent views that comprise our world's most important debates.

Introducing Issues with Opposing Viewpoints simplifies for students the enormous and often overwhelming mass of material now available via print and electronic media. Collected in every volume is an array of opinions that captures the essence of a particular controversy or topic. Introducing Issues with Opposing Viewpoints books embody the spirit of nineteenth-century journalist Charles A. Dana's axiom: "Fight for your opinions, but do not believe that they contain the whole truth, or the only truth." Absorbing such contrasting opinions teaches students to analyze the strength of an argument and compare it to its opposition. From this process readers can inform and strengthen their own opinions, or be exposed to new information that will change their minds. Introducing Issues with Opposing Viewpoints is a mosaic of different voices. The authors are statesmen, pundits, academics, journalists, corporations, and ordinary people who have felt compelled to share their experiences and ideas in a public forum. Their words have been collected from newspapers, journals, books, speeches, interviews, and the Internet, the fastest growing body of opinionated material in the world.

Introducing Issues with Opposing Viewpoints shares many of the well-known features of its critically acclaimed parent series, Opposing Viewpoints. The articles are presented in a pro/con format, allowing readers to absorb divergent perspectives side by side. Active reading questions preface each viewpoint, requiring the student to approach the material thoughtfully and carefully. Useful charts, graphs, and cartoons supplement each article. A thorough introduction provides readers with crucial background on an issue. An annotated bibliography points the reader toward articles, books, and websites that contain additional information on the topic. An appendix of organizations to contact contains a wide variety of charities, nonprofit organizations, political groups, and private enterprises that each hold a position on the issue at hand. Finally, a comprehensive index allows readers to locate content quickly and efficiently.

Introducing Issues with Opposing Viewpoints is also significantly different from Opposing Viewpoints. As the series title implies, its presentation will help introduce students to the concept of opposing viewpoints and learn to use this material to aid in critical writing and debate. The series' four-color, accessible format makes the books attractive and inviting to readers of all levels. In addition, each viewpoint has been carefully edited to maximize a reader's understanding of the content. Short but thorough viewpoints capture the essence of an argument. A substantial, thought-provoking essay question placed at the end of each viewpoint asks the student to further investigate the issues raised in the viewpoint, compare and contrast two authors' arguments, or consider how one might go about forming an opinion on the topic at hand. Each viewpoint contains sidebars that include at-a-glance information and handy statistics. A Facts About section located in the back of the book further supplies students with relevant facts and figures.

Following in the tradition of the Opposing Viewpoints series, Greenhaven Press continues to provide readers with invaluable exposure to the controversial issues that shape our world. As John Stuart Mill once wrote: "The only way in which a human being can make some approach to knowing the whole of a subject is by hearing what can be said about it by persons of every variety of opinion and studying all modes in which it can be looked at by every character of mind. No wise man ever acquired his wisdom in any mode but this." It is to this principle that Introducing Issues with Opposing Viewpoints books are dedicated.

Introduction

"Media have tremendous power in setting cultural guidelines and in shaping political discourse. It is essential that news media, along with other institutions, are challenged to be fair and accurate."

—Fairness and Accuracy in Reporting, "How to Detect Bias in News Media." www.fair.org.

The US public regularly charges the media with claims of biased news coverage. Data from the Pew Research Center for the People and the Press show that 66 percent of the public believe news stories are often inaccurate, and 77 percent believe news organizations usually favor one side. Although the public believes the media are biased, some question whether this perception matches reality. David D'Alessio, a communications sciences professor at the University of Connecticut at Stamford, studied campaign news coverage over a sixty-year period. He found that reporting in favor of liberals is often balanced by reporting that is favorable to conservatives and that the media have no overarching slant in favor of any political view. D'Alessio is skeptical of individual claims of media bias because "the perception of media bias by individual persons is subjective," and "the evidence that people commonly cite as proof of bias often fails to provide an adequate basis for a conclusion of bias."[1]

If the media are not becoming increasingly biased, why does public trust in them remain low? In every year since 2005, research by the Gallup organization has shown that at least half of the US public has very little confidence in the mass media. Some attribute this trend to the growing number of media outlets—many of which are partisan—in addition to the increasing number of media-watchdog organizations. The more that the press is scrutinized, the more the public sees a problem with media coverage. "Balanced media content is often perceived as biased," says Scott Reid, an associate professor in the Department of Communication at the University of California, Santa Barbara. Reid attributes this to the "hostile media effect," which is "a phenomenon in which partisans on both sides of an issue perceive neutral media reports to be biased against their side."[2]

One example of the hostile media effect is the issue of gun control in the United States. In 2012 a gunman killed twenty schoolchildren in a violent rampage at Sandy Hook Elementary School in Newtown, Connecticut. This was the third-deadliest mass killing in US history, according to the History News Network. The shooting sparked a national discussion about gun control, which has provoked activists on both sides to claim that the media are biased.

Gun rights activists charge that the media have used massacres such as the Newtown shooting in order to advance a liberal agenda for gun control. In a 2013 article for the Media Research Center, for example, Geoffrey Dickens, the center's deputy research director, says:

> In the wake of the horrific school shooting in Newtown, Connecticut on December 14, the Big Three (ABC, CBS, NBC) networks quickly moved to exploit the tragedy to push for more gun control legislation while mostly ignoring solutions that respect gun owners' Second Amendment rights. . . . The harsh truth is those brave police officers who have sworn to protect us, including the most innocent, like those children at Sandy Hook, can't always be everywhere, all the time. And sometimes it's up to private citizens to protect themselves and others by exercising their Second Amendment right, a fact that our Founding Fathers profoundly understood and sadly too many in the liberal media do not.[3]

Meanwhile, those on the opposite side of the debate believe that the media are not reporting the full story on gun control and are too lenient toward powerful gun rights groups such as the National Rifle Association (NRA). Journalist John Nichols believes that public support for the gun-safety movement is on the rise, yet the media reporting on the topic does not reflect this trend. In a January 2013 article in *The Nation*, Nichols writes:

> Too much coverage since the Newtown shootings in December has been deferential to the NRA—as if the group was somehow the victim. . . . The NRA must be covered, and it must be covered fairly. But honest coverage of the gun debate can and

should place the NRA in perspective. And that means the NRA's pronouncements should be balanced with coverage of the gun-safety groups that appear to be far more in touch with popular sentiment in the aftermath of the Newtown shootings.[4]

Whether the media are biased in their coverage of gun control is one of the many topics explored in *Introducing Issues with Opposing Viewpoints: Media Bias*. In the following chapters, authors debate the state of media bias in the United States. Some are adamant in their belief that media bias is a serious problem, while others question whether slanted media coverage has that much of an impact on society at all. Pro/con article pairs examine several high-profile issues and debate how media coverage plays a role in public perception of events. In addition, authors offer numerous arguments for how society can reduce bias in the media. Along with the article pairs, guided reading questions and essay prompts encourage readers to develop their own views on this highly contested topic.

Notes

1. Dave D'Alessio, *Media Bias in Presidential Election Coverage, 1948–2008: Evaluation via Formal Measurement*. Lanham, MD: Lexington Books, 2012, pp. 4–5.
2. Scott A. Reid, "A Self-Categorization Explanation for the Hostile Media Effect," *Journal of Communication*, June 2012, pp. 381–99.
3. Geoffrey Dickens, "ABC, CBS, NBC Slant 8 to 1 for Obama's Gun Control Crusade," Media Research Center, February 5, 2013. www.mrc.org/media-reality-check/abc-cbs-nbc-slant-8-1-obamas-gun-control-crusade.
4. John Nichols, "How Obsequious Media Coverage Perpetuates NRA Mythology," blog, *The Nation*, January 15, 2013. www.thenation.com/blog/172226/isnt-it-time-media-reset-gun-debate.

Chapter 1

Is Media Bias a Serious Problem?

Media bias is the imparting of a certain ideology—whether liberal, conservative, or somewhere on the spectrum— into the dissemination of news.

Viewpoint 1

The Media Are Biased

Tom Knighton

In the following viewpoint, Tom Knighton argues that the media are inherently biased. He examines the nature of the journalism industry and how it tends to attract young, idealistic reporters. Media bias becomes institutionalized, Knighton contends, as these young idealistic reporters move up in the industry and make decisions about what stories are covered and how the articles are structured. There is no such thing as an unbiased journalist, Knighton asserts, but consumers can fight institutionalized media bias by choosing which publications to support. Knighton is the publisher for the *Albany Journal*, an online newspaper in Albany, Georgia, and an assistant editor for *United Liberty*, a libertarian blog dedicated to examining public policy and current events.

> *"Media bias is very real."*

AS YOU READ, CONSIDER THE FOLLOWING QUESTIONS:

1. According to the author, what type of people usually pursue careers in industries with low pay?
2. As stated by Knighton, what motivates the career choices of libertarians or conservatives who want to change the world?
3. What happens to the careers of conservatives and libertarians who enter the journalism industry, according to the author?

A
sking about media bias is usually a good way to sniff out where someone falls on the political spectrum. If they run progressive, they probably don't think it exists. If they're a conservative or libertarian, they most likely believe it's a very real thing. Well, as a journalist, I'm here to tell you that it is.

Folks, media bias is real. There's no way to get around it, despite what your local newspaper reporter may say. It is real, and there are real reasons why it exists.

US Public Sees Media as Too Liberal

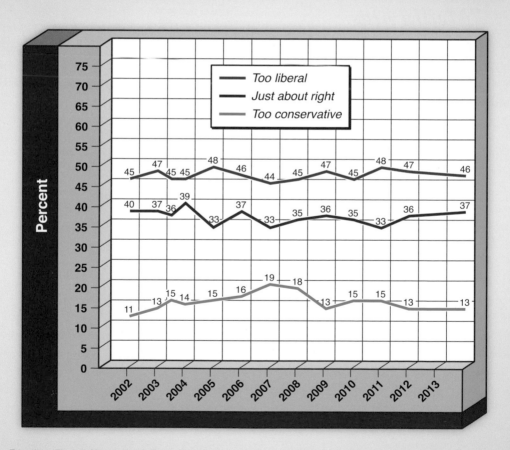

Taken from: Elizabeth Mendes, "In US, Trust in Media Recovers Slightly from All-Time Low," Gallup, September 19, 2013. www.gallup.com.

Why Media Bias Exists

First, journalism isn't a high paying position. While some journalists make good money, those are the ones at the top of the game. The very highest echelon of any industry tends to be rewarded greatly for that status, and journalism is no different. An industry with a lack of high paying jobs attracts a certain sort of person, and that's where the problem begins.

You see, the kind of people who tend to pursue a career in an industry that offers low pay are the kind of people who are extremely idealistic. That idealism is often translated as "I want to make the world a better place." There's nothing wrong with that on the surface, but if you scratch below the surface, you find a different matter.

FAST FACT

The Bureau of Labor Statistics reports that the mean annual wage for reporters and correspondents in the United States in 2013 was $44,360.

How Idealism Impacts the Journalism Field

These types of people are those who want to change the world for the better, and tend to lean left politically. Libertarians or conservatives who want to change the world tend to head into different professions, often ones that also offer the possibility of financial reward. Those few conservatives and libertarians who seek journalism careers are either out to right the wrongs of a left-leaning media, or they're masochists. Count me in the latter category.

So, year after year, you get more and more of these young, idealistic reporters leaving school and entering the workforce. Unsurprisingly, they seek employment in the field they actually studied.

Now that these new reporters are working, this is where their own biases start to come out. It's clear in a number of ways, including how a report is structured. For example, if they quote a gun control group early in the report, and then follow up with a gun rights group's response, a rebuttal by the gun control group at the end shows that the journalist isn't a fan of the Second Amendment. They honestly believe they presented an unbiased report since they gave both sides a voice, but that's not the case.

Their use of words is another way to slant it. For example, one man's "maverick" is another's "radical." The first term predisposes the reader to think of someone who stays the course, regardless of peer pressure. The second term suggests a nut job that makes bombs

A man is interviewed by CNN, a TV news network that is sometimes accused of having a liberal bias.

in his basement. However, as in the case of the structure, the reporter believes they've been unbiased.

To make matters worse, these young reporters often become veteran reporters, then editors and publishers. At that point, they decide the direction of newspapers and television news departments. The kicker? At no point are they actually lying when they say they're presenting unbiased news. After all, a lie requires them to actually know they're telling something that is untrue.

Media Bias Is Institutionalized

Media bias is very real, but it's also institutionalized through generations upon generations of reporters. Today, conservative and libertarian journalists are either run out of the industry, pushed to the realms of punditry where they can easily be ignored by those who don't share their ideology, or left to eventually seek asylum at conservative or libertarian news agencies of which there is a profound lack. After all, there's only so many job openings at Fox News and the *Wall Street Journal*.

Is there hope? Only the hope of the free market. More and more newspapers are failing, in part because of this bias. If you don't buy the newspaper as a reader, then advertisers won't buy space to try and sell you things. It doesn't make any sense for them to do so. A lack of advertising sales will kill any newspaper since that is where their real revenue comes from.

If that dwindles, as it has been for years, then eventually those papers will close their doors. Those that you support? They'll keep going, and the reporters will learn from the error of their ways. However, there still won't be any such thing as an unbiased reporter.

EVALUATING THE AUTHOR'S ARGUMENTS:

In this viewpoint, Tom Knighton maintains that media bias is institutionalized through generations of reporters. Do you agree with his assertion that utilizing the free market is the solution to fighting media bias? Why or why not?

How Biased Are the Media, Really?

Paul Farhi

"Left-leaning reporting is balanced by reporting more favorable to conservatives."

In the following viewpoint, Paul Farhi argues that the media are not biased. Although the public believes that media bias is on the rise, the author maintains that there is no evidence to support this perception. Researchers have found biased reporting, Farhi asserts, but they have not found that one side is consistently favored or that media bias is increasing. The author believes the public perceives a rise in media bias because there are more media to consume, and this increases the chances of encountering news that appears slanted. In addition, he contends, there are more media watchdog groups, which have heightened the awareness of media bias. Farhi is a media reporter for the *Washington Post*.

AS YOU READ, CONSIDER THE FOLLOWING QUESTIONS:

1. According to the author, what percentage of the public believes that the media are biased?
2. According to a study by researcher David D'Alessio, as cited by Farhi, are the US news media more liberal or conservative?
3. What percentage of the public believes that the news media are often inaccurate, according to the author?

J ust about every new poll of public sentiment shows that confidence in the news media has hit a new low. Seventy-seven percent of those surveyed by the Pew Research Center in the fall [of 2011] said the media "tend to favor one side" compared with 53 percent who said so in 1985.

But have the media really become more biased? Or is this a case of perception trumping reality?

In fact, there's little to suggest that over the past few decades news reporting has become more favorable to one party. That's not to say researchers haven't found bias in reporting. They have, but they don't agree that one side is consistently favored or that this favoritism has been growing like a pernicious weed.

Analyzing Media Bias

On the conservative side, the strongest case might have been made by Tim Groseclose, a political science and economics professor at the University of California at Los Angeles. Groseclose used a three-

Research suggests that people think the news sources they trust are relatively unbiased, while other news sources—ones they do not watch or read—are very biased.

pronged test to quantify the "slant quotient" of news stories reported by dozens of media sources. He compared these ratings with a statistical analysis of the voting records of various national politicians. In his 2011 book, *Left Turn: How Liberal Bias Distorts the American Mind*, Groseclose concluded that most media organizations aligned with the views of liberal politicians. (Groseclose determined that the *Washington Post*'s "slant quotient" was less liberal than news coverage in the *New York Times* and *Wall Street Journal*.)

Even with conservative-leaning sources such as the Drudge Report and the *Washington Times* factored in, "the aggregate slant is leftward," said Groseclose, who describes himself as a conservative.

But that's not the end of the story. A "meta-analysis" of bias studies—that is, a study of studies—shows something different: When all is said and done, left-leaning reporting is balanced by reporting more favorable to conservatives. "The net effect is zero," said David D'Alessio, a communications sciences professor at the University of Connecticut at Stamford.

D'Alessio drew his conclusion from reviewing 99 studies of campaign news coverage undertaken over six decades for his newly published work, *Media Bias in Presidential Election Coverage 1948–2008: Evaluation via Formal Measurement*. The research, he says, shows that news reporting tends to point toward the middle, "because that's where the people are, and that's where the [advertising] money is. . . . There's nuance there, but when you add it all and subtract it down, you end up with nothing."

Why the Public Perceives a Rise in Media Bias

So why the rise in the public's perception of media bias? A few possibilities:

The media landscape has changed.

There's more media and more overtly partisan media outlets, too. The Internet has given rise to champions of the left—*Huffington Post*, Daily Kos, etc.—as well as more conservative organizations such as Drudge and Free Republic. This means your chance of running into "news" that seems biased has increased exponentially, elevating the impression that "bias" is pervasive throughout all parts of the media.

"There's a kind of self-fulfilling perception to it," said Robert Lichter, a pioneering media-bias researcher who heads the Center for Media and Public Affairs at George Mason University. "Once people see something they don't like, they notice things that reinforce the belief that there's bias" in the media as a whole.

There are more watchdog groups focused on rooting out media bias.

Long ago, a few watchdog groups, such as the conservative AIM (Accuracy in Media) and its more liberal counterpart FAIR (Fairness and Accuracy in Reporting), kept an eye on reporters' work. Nowadays, not just politicians criticize the media for their alleged bias; an entire cottage industry exists to highlight the media's alleged failings. This includes ideological outfits such as Media Matters for America and the Media Research Center; the satirical *Daily Show* and *Colbert Report*; and blogs by the hundreds.

All that scrutiny of the press may suggest an inescapable conclusion: There's something wrong with the news media. All the time.

Journalists have gotten that message, too. "Reporters have heard the criticism from the right so often that they lean over backwards to be fair to them," said Eric Alterman, a journalist, college professor and the author of the best-selling *What Liberal Media? The Truth About Bias and the News.*

> # FAST FACT
>
> According to the Pew Research Center, 63 percent of survey respondents believe that the news media are politically biased in their reporting.

In the public's mind, "the news media" encompasses the kitchen sink.

Few people make a distinction between news reporting—which attempts to play it straight—and opinion-mongering, which is designed to provoke and persuade. Tellingly, when asked what they

The Increase in Negative Evaluations of Press Performance

Percent of respondents saying that the press . . .

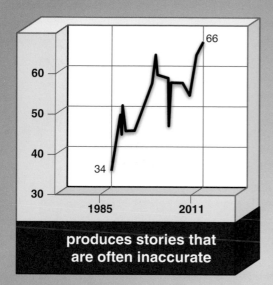

**produces stories that
are often inaccurate**

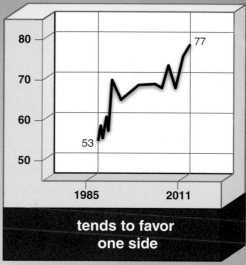

**tends to favor
one side**

**is often influenced by powerful
people and organizations**

Taken from: Pew Research Center for the People and the Press, "Press Widely Criticized, but Trusted More than Other Information Sources,"
September 22, 2011. www.people-press.org.

think of when they hear the phrase "news organization," the majority of respondents (63 percent) in Pew's news-bias survey cited "cable news," and specifically Fox News and CNN. But while cable news networks do some straightforward reporting, their most popular programs, by far, are those in which opinionated hosts ask opinionated guests to sling opinions about the day's news.

"A big part of the conversation on cable is [people] telling you how the rest of the media is getting the story wrong," said Mark Jurkowitz, a former press critic and newspaper ombudsman who is now associate director of the Project for Excellence in Journalism, a Washington-based research group affiliated with Pew. That, he noted, is likely to sow more doubt about the media's integrity or accuracy.

Of course, reporters have helped blur the very lines they want the public to respect, Lichter said, by writing up news stories and then appearing on TV or going on social media to tell people what to think about their stories.

"The modern way [for journalists] is to be edgy and opinionated and to call attention to yourself," Lichter said.

We know more and can second-guess.

Thanks to technology, people have more access to more sources of news than before. Which means they can check several accounts of the same event. This can create its own kind of suspicion; savvy readers often ask reporters why they ignored or played down facts that another reporter emphasized.

People believe their preferred news sources are objective and fair, while the other guy's are biased.

Pew's research suggests that people think the other guy's media are spreading lies while one's own are, relatively, a paragon of truth.

A clear majority (66 percent) say news organizations in general are "often inaccurate." But the figure drops precipitously (to 30 percent) when people are asked the same question about the news organization "you use most." Jurkowitz said this is the analogue of how people feel about Congress—most give low marks to lawmakers in general, but they vote to reelect their incumbent representative more than 90 percent of the time.

"If you watch the Channel 2 newscast night after night, you trust the people on the air," he said. "The mere fact that you're a habituated user makes you think better of them."

Despite the low esteem the public seems to hold for "the news media," the good news may be that it's all relative. Pew found last year that people said they trusted information from the news media more than any other source, including state governments, the Obama administration, federal government agencies, corporations and Congress.

The lowest degree of trust? By far, people named "candidates running for office."

EVALUATING THE AUTHOR'S ARGUMENTS:

In this viewpoint, Paul Farhi asserts that the public perceives an increase in media bias but that there is no evidence to support this belief. Who has a more convincing argument about media bias, Farhi or Tom Knighton, author of the previous viewpoint? Why? Provide a piece of evidence or quote that had an impact on your opinion.

Viewpoint
3

Media Bias Is Difficult to Judge

Tim Groseclose

"The problem is that our opinions . . . are based almost entirely upon information we learn from the media"

In the following viewpoint, Tim Groseclose argues that analyzing media bias is a difficult process because the beliefs of viewers/readers determine which media sources they find trustworthy. This makes it hard for viewers/readers to accurately detect biased media because their perception is already influenced by their personal views. In addition, Groseclose contends, the public gets most of its information about the world from the media, which further blurs the ability to determine biased media. He outlines several factors that impact the public's judgment of the media and offers methods for analyzing media bias. Groseclose is a professor of political science and economics at the University of California, Los Angeles.

AS YOU READ, CONSIDER THE FOLLOWING QUESTIONS:

1. According to the author, how does circular thinking impact one's ability to identify media bias?
2. What is the difference between relative bias and absolute bias, in Groseclose's opinion?
3. Why is the fundamental trap worse for those who are more informed, according to the author?

Tim Groseclose, *Left Turn: How Liberal Media Bias Distorts the American Mind.* New York: St. Martin's Griffin, 2012, pp. 18–25. Copyright © 2011 by Tim Groseclose. Reprinted by permission of Palgrave Macmillan. All Rights Reserved.

All of us base our political views to a large degree, on information we learn from the media. Of course, we trust some media sources more than others. So we are careful to filter out the untrustworthy sources from the trustworthy ones. The problem is that our political views often determine which media outlets we consider trustworthy or untrustworthy. Thus, our thinking is circular: our political views influence where we go for news, which influences our political views, which further influences where we go for news, and so on.

The circularity makes our political views flimsy. That is, for instance a little bit of liberal media bias can make us more liberal, which causes us to seek more liberal media outlets, which causes us to become more liberal and so on.

The circularity also makes us bad at judging and detecting media bias, and often we don't realize how bad at it we are. As an example, consider the following hypothetical conversation, which is only a slight caricature of perhaps dozens that I have had with fellow political science professors.

> *Me:* The evidence is clear that the mainstream media cite left-wing think tanks more than they cite right-wing ones.
>
> *Colleague:* Yes, but that's because experts at left-wing think tanks tend to be more respected and scholarly, while the experts at right-wing think tanks tend to be hired guns for corporations. The media are not showing a left-wing bias, only a bias for respected and scholarly experts.
>
> *Me:* But how do you know that left-wing experts are more respected and scholarly than right-wing experts?
>
> *Colleague:* Just read or watch any reputable news source. It's well documented. . . .

The Fundamental Trap in Judging Media Bias

The circularities in such arguments are examples of what I call the *Fundamental Trap* of judging media bias. To determine if the media

In general, how much trust and confidence do you have in the mass media—such as newspapers, TV, and radio—when it comes to reporting the news fully, accurately, and fairly: a great deal, a fair amount, not very much, or none at all?

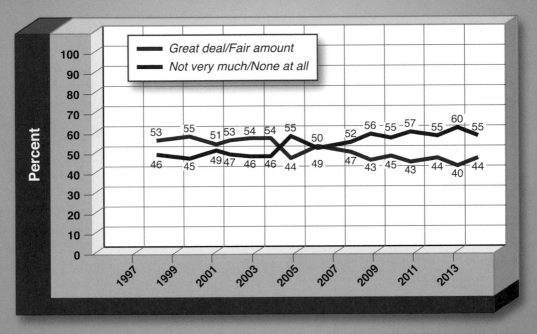

Taken from: Elizabeth Mendes, "In US, Trust in Media Recovers Slightly from All-Time Low," Gallup, September 19, 2013. www.gallup.com.

are biased, we need an accurate and unbiased source of information. But almost all of us, on almost any political topic, must rely on the media as our main source of information. We rarely have other sources. . . . Consider the question "To what extent do guns deter burglars from entering our homes?" Almost none of us has any direct knowledge about this question. That is, few of us have ever interviewed a burglar, much less peered inside his head to see if his burglary decisions were influenced by whether his next victim might own a gun. Instead, almost all of our knowledge on this topic comes from what we read, watch, or hear from the media.

Now consider the question "How many stories should the media report about guns doing good, say, thwarting a burglary, versus stories about guns doing harm, say, causing an accidental death?"

First, we can all agree that the media cannot report all the stories where a gun has done harm or good. There are simply not enough minutes in a newscast, nor pages in a newspaper. We can also agree that the number of stories should reflect the truth—that is, the stories should reflect the proportion of the two types of cases that actually occur in the world. For example, if, in the universe of all cases, a gun does good 30 percent of the time and harm 70 percent of the time, then, in an ideal journalistic world, 30 percent of the media's gun stories would be about a gun doing good and 70 percent about a gun doing harm.

Of course, no one knows the actual percentage of cases in which guns do good or harm. The best we can do is form opinions and educated guesses about the true percentage. The problem is that our opinions and educated guesses are based almost entirely upon information we learn from the media. Accordingly, how can we know how accurate are our educated guesses and opinions? And if we cannot know this, how can we judge how biased or unbiased the media are?

To take the argument to the extreme, suppose that the media were your only source of knowledge. Then they could be extremely biased, and you would never know it. It would be as if your only information about the world came from watching professional basketball games. If so, then you would think that six foot eight was a normal height, and six-three was short. Further, you would have no idea that your primary source of information about the world, televised basketball games, was giving you a distorted picture of the true distribution of people's heights.

The analogy illustrates another point about judging the media: People often mistake bias, relative to other media outlets, as an absolute bias. That is, for instance, Fox News is clearly more conservative than ABC, CBS, CNN, NBC, and National Public Radio. Some will conclude that "therefore, this means that Fox News has a conservative bias." But this says nothing about its bias on any absolute scale. Instead, maybe it is centrist, and possibly even left-leaning, while all the others are far left. It is like concluding that six-three is short just because it is short compared to professional basketball players. . . . Although most of us think we can accurately judge which media outlets are conservative, which are liberal, and so on, we should all ask ourselves, "Are we basing this upon any outside source of information—that is, on anything besides what we've learned from the media?" If not, we are no different from the person judging people's heights from watching basketball games.

Alpha Intellectuals' Vulnerability to the Fundamental Trap

Many people would respond to my argument as follows: "While plausible, the Fundamental Trap does not affect me, since I am better informed and more educated than most people." In some ways, however, the trap is even worse for these people, since, more than average people, they tend to base their worldviews on knowledge from the media, instead of outside sources such as personal experience and conversations with friends.

The extreme form of the latter-type person is what I call an *alpha intellectual*. Such a person is highly educated, or at least considers himself highly educated. He spends much time reading and watching the news, and he has convinced himself, to the point of near certainty, that his media sources are the most "highly respected" and "trustworthy" of all sources. As a consequence, he dismisses other sources, particularly media-independent sources of information, and especially media-independent sources who are not as highly educated or as well informed as he considers himself. Like an alpha male in an animal tribe, he is sometimes boorish if someone mentions a fact that contradicts his "highly respected" and "trustworthy" sources. . . . In defining the notion of alpha intellectual, let me make two clarifications: First, I don't believe that anyone is a pure alpha intellectual. We all are partial alpha intellectuals. Consequently, our political beliefs will be partially influenced by media bias, and we will be partially oblivious to that

A variety of news outlets cover the same incident in Washington, DC, in 2006. For most viewers, media bias is difficult to detect because they choose to watch or read sources they believe to be trustworthy.

bias. Further, the two factors will still feed off of each other; however, instead of our beliefs wandering continually further and further from the truth, the wandering will be finite—albeit possibly a very far distance from the truth. . . . My point is that if the media are your only, or almost only, source of information, and if you rarely learn anything from personal experience or any other media-independent sources of information, then you are stuck in the trap. You will trust the media simply because what they say is consistent with your beliefs, which are based upon what you have learned from the media. You might get lucky—the media might be truly unbiased—but if they are biased and presenting an inaccurate picture of the world, then you will never learn that.

How to Escape the Fundamental Trap

The key to avoiding the Fundamental Trap is to find a source of information that is independent of the media and also independent of the personal beliefs of the analyst judging the media. This may seem difficult, but it can be done.

One excellent example is a [2004] study by [economists] John Lott and Kevin Hassett. They analyze newspaper headlines that focus on economic news, specifically unemployment, GDP [gross national product] growth, durable goods production, and retail sales. They note whether a given headline describes the news in a positive or negative fashion, and they analyze whether the media outlet's choice was related to whether the president was Republican or Democrat.

One noteworthy aspect of the study is that it documents a well-kept secret in journalism: two media outlets covering the exact same story can use vastly different headlines to describe it.

At this point, if you are a careful reader, you should sense that the Fundamental Trap potentially applies to the Lott-Hassett study. That is, there is no reason for journalists necessarily to describe economic conditions under Democrat and Republican presidents equally. That is, for instance, economies under Democratic administrations might in general perform better than economies under Republican administrations. If so, then a newspaper should describe them asymmetrically.

But if "unbiased" does not necessarily mean symmetric, then how should a journalist, or a researcher of media bias, decide upon the proper degree of asymmetry? After all, won't the judgments of Lott and Hassett regarding whether a headline should be positive or negative be colored by what they have read or heard in the news?

Yes, but here's the most brilliant aspect of their study . . . and the way they escape the Fundamental Trap. Lott and Hassett focus only on stories where the underlying news is an objective piece of data, which does not come from the media. They then construct a statistical technique that explicitly controls for these data. Most important, their assessment, whether the economy is good or bad, does not rely on their own judgment and intuition.

Lott and Hassett indeed find a liberal bias in the media. They find that for the same piece of news, major U.S. newspapers are 20 to 40 percent more likely to report a negative headline if the administration is Republican than if it is Democratic.

At least for now, however, the details of their conclusions are unimportant. What is important is that the Lott-Hassett study demonstrates that it really is possible to measure media bias while avoiding the Fundamental Trap.

EVALUATING THE AUTHOR'S ARGUMENTS:

In this viewpoint, Tim Groseclose details the difference between relative bias and absolute bias. Do you believe it is important for the public to understand the differences between the two biases in order to analyze media content? Explain.

Does Media Bias Matter?

Chris Ladd

"Does the liberal lean of the journalistic establishment matter?"

In the following viewpoint, Chris Ladd argues that journalism is traditionally based on liberal values; however, Ladd questions whether the ideology of the journalism industry presents a problem for society. The liberal values of objectivity and doubt prevent journalism from turning into propaganda, the author contends. Therefore, journalism's liberal bent does not prevent the industry from offering a useful contribution to society because, the author maintains, an institution can have an ideological bent without compromising its effectiveness. Ladd is the author of the *Houston Chronicle*'s *GOPlifer* blog.

AS YOU READ, CONSIDER THE FOLLOWING QUESTIONS:

1. According to the author, what are the liberal values of the journalism profession?
2. What change in society intensified the conflict between conservatives and the news media, as stated by Ladd?
3. According to the author, why do religious conservatives believe the news media have a liberal bias?

Certain institutions have an inherent ideological lean. There aren't a lot of vegans in the Marine Corps. You won't find many Ayn Rand enthusiasts working at child protective services. Likewise, journalism as a profession offers little that would appeal to the average conservative.

It's no secret that most reporters are politically liberal, but does that compromise their work? Getting to an answer requires understanding the mission of journalism and its relationship to conservative values.

Being a conservative in the traditional meaning of the word means, to paraphrase Russell Kirk, a belief in a transcendent order based in tradition and nature. In the conservative understanding of the world, we are more than the sum of our parts. Conservatives generally admire traditional institutions and tend to emphasize faith, rather than skepticism, as a core value. Conservatives don't dismiss science or provable facts, but they humbly place what we learn from science inside a wider perspective.

Journalism, on the other hand, is based on traditionally liberal values. A reporter's mission is to uncover truth based on observable, proven facts, free from the influence of faith, tradition, or other subjective factors. Reporters have a mission to challenge authority and scrutinize what others regard as sacred. Journalism is an ideology as much as a profession.

In short, good journalists embrace liberal values in their work.

For generations this clash of values fed friction between the professional news media and conservatives. The right often viewed reporters as a corps of professional turd-disturbers unwilling to let well enough alone. To conservatives, journalists' aggressive skepticism leads to a consistent failure to see the bigger picture. Their narrow focus makes them suckers for a sob story and vulnerable to manipulation.

That said, apart from extreme instances (see "McCarthy, Joe"), until recently you seldom heard conservatives attacking the profession directly. For decades the right questioned the completeness of the news media's narratives, as with Nixon's "Silent Majority" theme, but they did it without attempting to replace fact-based reality with some ideological alternative.

The global rise of religious fundamentalism changed the conservative movement in the U.S. and brought new intensity to its conflict with the news media. Fundamentalists are far more deeply at odds

"*Even when public television deals with astronomy, one can detect a liberal tilt.*"

with the journalistic philosophy than traditional conservatives ever were. The missions of journalism and political religion clash harshly because they lay conflicting claims to truth.

To religious conservatives, the news media's exclusive reliance on observable reality is itself a bias. It conflicts directly with their belief that truth is revealed to them not by science or inquiry but by God alone, superior to and beyond objective analysis. Unlike traditional conservatives, the religious far right sees their political rivals as agents of a deep, spiritual evil. By that standard, modern journalism is little more than professional deception.

That's why fact-checking Michele Bachmann is such an absurd and pointless exercise. You either share her understanding of received reality or you don't. Subjecting her claims to a scientifically inspired analysis is to hold her to a standard that she rejects.

Journalists start with skepticism, then determine reality based on discovered facts. Fundamentalists start from certainty, filtering observed reality through an ideological lens to protect their faith.

The journalistic establishment was horrified and baffled when a Bush Administration official derided them as lowly members of the "reality-based community." The comedian Steven Colbert clarified that critique when he joked that "reality has a well-known liberal bias." In the emerging global rivalry between political religion and objective reality, that statement might be uncontroversial on both sides.

Does the liberal lean of the journalistic establishment matter? The answer hinges on the fragility of one's beliefs. Traditional conservatism was never threatened by journalism. Conservatism may claim to be bigger than reported facts, but it is never endangered by them.

Traditional conservatives accept a reporter's interpretation as a useful contribution to a wider picture. Science and reason provide a frame of reference, beyond which lie deeper truths. They see the news media as a valued, if limited, contributor to our understanding of events.

Journalism's inherent liberal lean is not a bug, it's a feature. An institution can have an ideological bent without compromising its effectiveness. No one should expect great results from a liberal military or a conservative university. It is possible to build a conservative news media, but it's not a good idea. Without the emphasis on liberal

FAST FACT

A 2008 Pew Research Center report found that 32 percent of national journalists say they are liberals, while just 8 percent say they are conservatives. Only 19 percent of the US population considers itself liberal, while 36 percent considers itself conservative.

values of objectivity and relentless doubt, journalism quickly descends into propaganda.

However, for those who seek to impose on others a vision of reality revealed to them by the voices in their heads, journalism is more than an irritant. Whatever contradicts their brittle worldview is dangerous. For fundamentalists, the "lamestream media" is a lie factory. Its reliance on proof springs from its rejection of righteous revelation.

Under the influence of religious fundamentalism the right is finding itself at odds not just with reporters, but with the whole concept of provable reality. From evolution to history to climate science, the religious right is pushing the conservative movement and the Republican Party toward a declaration of independence from facts. A political philosophy that withers in the daylight of honest inquiry has problems more serious than the news media.

EVALUATING THE AUTHOR'S ARGUMENTS:

In this viewpoint, Chris Ladd argues that the journalism industry has an ideological bias, but this is inherent in its nature and does not harm society. Do you agree with his assertion that the media can be biased and still be effective? Why or why not?

Viewpoint

5

Media Bias Reflects the Desires of Consumers

Emiley Conboy and Lindsay Hoffman

"We seek media outlets that appeal to our own ideological compass."

In the following viewpoint, the authors examine the relationship between political identities and media bias. They believe that the ability of the public to interpret the news has been influenced by the increase of cable news networks, online media, and opinion reporting. The media have become more polarized, which has led to an increased ideological distance among the public. The authors maintain that increasingly polarized media allow the public to consume filtered news and so remain unaware of opposing thoughts and views. They argue that the public needs to question whether its consumption patterns have forced the media to cater to a closed-minded demographic. At the time this viewpoint was written, Emiley Conboy was a political science major at the University of Delaware, where Lindsay Hoffman is an associate professor of communication.

AS YOU READ, CONSIDER THE FOLLOWING QUESTIONS:
1. According to the authors, why is the news now more open to interpretation?
2. As stated in the viewpoint, what percentage of CNN programming is opinion reporting?
3. What is the running tally theory, according to the authors?

Lately, steering clear of religion and politics at dinner parties seems a wise way to live. Deadlocked political opinions and the disappearance of the elusive Moderate may have less to do with an increasingly argumentative electorate, and more to do with the nature of the media and our own personal political identification.

While one can make the argument that media economics has led to less diversity and more prepackaged news, the rise of cable networks and various online outlets leaves news open to interpretation like never before. Long gone are the days of gathering around the television at night to hear one of the big three networks' nightly broadcasts

Critics say that, increasingly, news outlets such as Fox News and MSNBC interpret the news to suit their viewers' political ideologies rather than report the news.

in which the choice of B-roll [secondary] material may be the only distinguishing factor. Americans now have a "home base" of sorts, to which they turn for all of their news, and as a result, their opinions.

Framing has proved to be a powerful tool in shaping the views of the electorate. What's important is not always the story itself, but how the story is told. All it takes is a quick toggle between MSNBC and Fox for it to become apparent that there are many sides to the same issues. Feeling disenfranchised by uppity corporate America? The liberal slant of MSNBC's Rachel Maddow may be for you. Tired of the socialist hippie idealists? You may want a serving of *Fox and Friends* with your morning coffee.

Opinion Reporting Affects Media Consumers

In 2012, Pew Research Center's Project for Excellence in Journalism found that CNN, Fox, and MSNBC all had 46, 55, and 85% opinion reporting, respectively. When this much of cable news information has diverted from hard facts, it is bound [to] have an effect on viewers.

These polarizations in the media are only leading to increased ideological distance among the electorate. Talking points, political knowledge, and an idea of the most important issues of the day are gained from one's source of information. Purposeful filtering results in a public that is not only unaware of opposing thoughts and views, but will never be forced to confront them as a result of the increasingly diverse media.

The media function as interpreters of news, and socialize the electorate, which allows for liberty in reporting. The same story on two different news outlets could be presented so differently one could almost believe they were listening to two different series of events. Living in a world of instant gratification where how many "likes" something gets becomes a status symbol,

FAST FACT

According to research done by University of Texas at Austin faculty members, 64 percent of Republicans will routinely turn to at least one right-leaning media source for their news, while 76 percent of Democrats go to at least one left-leaning media source.

being vindicated is key in society. As a result, we seek media outlets that appeal to our own ideological compass. This type of gravitational sorting leaves the electorate not only polarized, but on two different pages entirely.

Ideology of News Program Audiences

Main source for news about government and politics for the largest percentage of the audience in each ideological group:

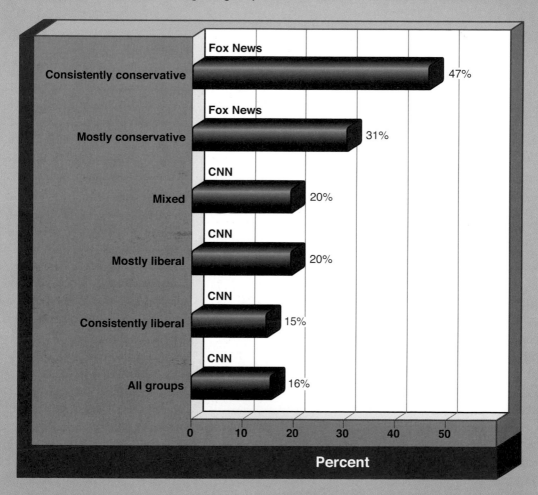

Taken from: Pew Research Center, "Political Polarization and Media Habits: From Fox News to Facebook, How Liberals and Conservatives Keep Up with Politics," October 21, 2014. www.journalism.org.

This "tale of two Americas" epidemic was especially apparent in the recent [2013] federal government shutdown. Being able to discern the true consequences of the shutdown was difficult. Fox news called the shutdown simply a "slim down," while opposing liberally slanted outlets were emphasizing the negative aspects of furloughed federal workers and runners not being able to take their daily jog in the local national park. I, like many Americans, rely on the media to tell me what is happening, so it is understandable that without a home base media outlet on which one's true faith rests, we would not only have a polarized electorate, but a very confused one.

Political Identification Influences Media Consumption

So why does one person rely on one news outlet and not another? It goes back to the issue of political identification. [University of Wisconsin–Green Bay assistant professor of political science] Aaron Weinschenk describes the running tally theory, which assumes that everyone starts out as a neutral palette and everything they hear about each party ads or subtracts from their opinion. Eventually people will settle on a position on the liberal–conservative scale as they collect more information.

This theory is an overly idealized concept of the capabilities of the electorate. [Indiana University–Bloomington political science professor] Marjorie Hershey demonstrates that political identifications take root surprisingly early in life. People are generally not interested in absorbing opinions from all sides and adjusting their political identity accordingly. Not only would this mean more work, but it may lead to a challenge of their long-established party preference. The reality is that we interpret information through a "partisan perceptual screen." . . . This suggests that all information one receives is filtered through already established beliefs. This could explain why there are so many news outlets that cater to a certain clientele. If people will discard any information that is not in line with their ideology, then why waste the time hearing any opposing views in the first place? Should one hear others' opinions, it may not be used to adjust one's political slant, instead it will be rationalized away or forgotten, as it does not fit with their screen.

So, which came first? Did the media become so individualized and then people realized they never had to hear an opposing opinion again? Or was it the inflexibility of the perceptual screen that forced the media to cater to a closed-minded demographic?

Next time you are trying to hold a political discussion with someone, there are two things working against the possibility of either you or your friend conceding: the highly partisan media of today, and the perceptual screen of our own political identification. The present media atmosphere means people can avoid hearing anything they don't want to. While the media serve as an easy target on which to cast blame for the trend of a polarized closed-minded populace, let's face it, they are only responding to what we all want.

EVALUATING THE AUTHORS' ARGUMENTS:

In this viewpoint, Emiley Conboy and Lindsay Hoffman claim that public demand has led to a polarized media culture. On the basis of what you have read, do you believe that the public has a desire for biased media? Explain your answer.

Chapter 2

How Does Media Bias Affect Society?

Members of Tea Party 365 and their supporters rally in front of the New York Times building in New York in 2010.

Viewpoint 1

Big-Business Ownership Causes Media Bias

Alison Langley

"Tycoons have been buying up media outlets and appearing to exert editorial control."

In the following viewpoint, Alison Langley argues that media ownership by business tycoons has an impact on media bias. The author asserts that there has been a trend throughout Europe of tycoons buying up media outlets and exerting editorial control. She contends that media are increasingly under the influence of owners with business interests other than media. When the media attempt real reporting, Langley maintains, they face consequences from government officials or powerful business entities. As a result, the author concludes, media in countries with a high concentration of tycoon ownership tend to keep their owners happy by covering safe topics such as sports and entertainment. Langley is a reporter and editor who has worked for the *New York Times*, *The Guardian*, the *Financial Times*, and *The Independent*. She also teaches journalism at Fachhochschule Wien and Webster University Vienna in Austria.

AS YOU READ, CONSIDER THE FOLLOWING QUESTIONS:

1. According to the author, which newspaper did Amazon CEO Jeff Bezos purchase?
2. As stated by Langley, how are corporate media owners different from earlier press barons?
3. What has happened to the media in eastern and southeastern Europe, according to Langley?

In 2010, the German media conglomerate WAZ sold its Bulgarian Media Group to two millionaire tycoons: Ognian I. Bonev, chairman and executive director of Bulgaria's biggest pharmaceutical company, and Lyubomir Pavlov, a former banker. Included in the purchase were two mass dailies, *24 Chassa* and *Trud*. The latter's longtime editor, Tosho Toshev, was promptly fired.

Soon after, Toshev published—in a different newspaper, owned by New Bulgarian Media Group—transcripts of alleged phone conversations that indicate Bonev and Pavlov have undue influence with leading political figures. A national TV station aired an investigation alleging that Pavlov used real estate he owned in the French Côte d'Azur to launder money.

None of these stories, which Pavlov and Bonev adamantly denied, appeared in any publication or station owned by Bulgarian Media Group. Instead, those outlets ran pieces alleging massive wrongdoing by New Bulgarian Media Group, believed to be controlled by a bank owner, although true ownership is unclear because of the way the group is structured.

FAST FACT

According to analysis by Freedom House, a human rights watchdog, 86 percent of the world's citizens in 2014 lived in countries where the press is not free or is only partially free.

Then there is Ivo Prokopiev, the money behind Bulgaria's third-largest media group, Economedia, as well as, until very recently, Kaolin mining group. While most of Bulgaria's media reported in 2012 that one of Kaolin's mines was polluting the drinking water in a nearby village, there [were] no such stories in Economedia-owned papers, according to a passage cited by Andrey Anastassov, a graduate student at Central European University.

Business Tycoons Are Buying Media Outlets

Although Bulgaria is an extreme example, it isn't the only European country in which tycoons have been buying up media outlets and appearing to exert editorial control. It has become common practice in Europe long before Amazon's Jeff Bezos decided to buy the *Washington Post*.

World Press Freedom Index

The press freedom index that Reporters Without Borders publishes every year measures the level of freedom of information in 180 countries. It reflects the degree of freedom that journalists, news organizations and netizens enjoy in each country, and the efforts made by the authorities to respect and ensure respect for this freedom.

TOP TEN		BOTTOM TEN	
Rank	Country	Rank	Country
1	Finland	171	Laos
2	Netherlands	172	Sudan
3	Norway	173	Iran
4	Luxembourg	174	Vietnam
5	Andorra	175	China
6	Liechtenstein	176	Somalia
7	Denmark	177	Syria
8	Iceland	178	Turkmenistan
9	New Zealand	179	North Korea
10	Sweden	180	Eritrea

Taken from: Reporters Without Borders, "World Press Freedom Index," February 2014. http://rsf.org.

"In virtually every country [in eastern and southeast Europe], those involved in media are also involved in other businesses. All of them influence editorial control or promote a political ideology," said Oliver Vujovic, secretary general of South East Europe Media Organization, a press watchdog.

Victor Pinchuk, a Ukrainian piping magnate, owns nearly all of his country's private TV stations, along with the wealthiest man in Ukraine, Rinat Akhmetov, who built his fortune in steel and coal, according to *Forbes*. In Turkey, media ownership is highly concentrated, and their owners do not hesitate to exert editorial control, according to Freedom House.

"This used to be limited to Eastern Europe," said Christoph Keese, spokesman for Germany's Axel Springer AG. "Now Germany is the

Billionaire Jeff Bezos bought the Washington Post Company (and its subsidiaries, including the Express *newspaper) in 2013. Some experts question whether a media outlet owned by a wealthy businessperson can remain impartial in its coverage of news stories.*

last big European market with no newspapers having been sold out to industrialists yet."

Indeed, over the last three years, wealthy tycoons have started buying up leading titles in western European countries like France and Spain. (Italy's media landscape has been long bought up by Silvio Berlusconi, who controlled the political debate, but that is a different story.)

Bernart Arnault, one of the richest men in the world, owns *Les Echos* in France. Nicolas Berggruen, the "homeless billionaire" who prefers to sleep in luxury hotels, bought a controlling interest in *El Pais* in Spain in 2010, just after he purchased a stake in *Le Monde*. All these publications were independently owned by media publishers before they were sold to businessmen with much wider arrays of interests.

As CJR's [*Columbia Journalism Review*] Dean Starkman puts it, these guys are different from earlier press barons, like James Gordon Bennett Sr. or Joseph Pulitzer. "The early press barons' power was generated by their newspaper businesses. That was the source of their wealth—the press itself. Their primary interest was the media business," Starkman wrote.

Tycoon Ownership Impacts Free Speech

Granted, even taking industrialist owners out of the free speech equation, the media landscape in eastern and southeastern Europe is anything but unfettered, in spite of laws officially guaranteeing a free press. But some of the crackdown on free speech appears to come from these owners rather than solely from the government. Where it is possible to discern ownership—shell companies with addresses in Cyprus or Bermuda can hide the true owners, said Vujovic, of the South East Europe Media Organization—newspapers, TV, and radio stations in eastern and southeastern Europe increasingly are under the influence of owners with business interests other than media and, usually, ties to the ruling government.

When media do attempt real reporting—say, a well-researched piece on some government wrongdoing—their publishers are threatened by government officials with, say, an extra business tax or revocation of an important contract. So they ask their editors to stop. This is especially true in Turkey, say press watchdogs like the Committee to Protect Journalists and Freedom House.

As a result, media in countries with a high concentration of tycoon ownership tend to keep their owners happy by covering safe topics, like sports and entertainment.

In western Europe and North America, there is a stronger tradition of free press. Attempts at manipulation are likely to be reported. Bezos has stated that he will not exercise editorial control. So far *Les Echos*, *Le Monde* and *El Pais* have remained independent.

Whether they will continue to be centers for hard-hitting, serious news may be another matter.

EVALUATING THE AUTHOR'S ARGUMENTS:

In this viewpoint, Alison Langley claims that tycoon media ownership has a direct impact on news coverage. How might someone argue that media ownership by non-media business owners does not lead to biased news coverage?

Viewpoint

2

Media Slant: A Question of Cause and Effect

N. Gregory Mankiw

"[Research- ers] find no correlation between the politi- cal slant of a paper and the owner's ideology."

In the following viewpoint, N. Gregory Mankiw questions whether media owner- ship has an impact on media bias. While it is often assumed that a media outlet's per- spective reflects the ideology of its owner, Mankiw says media ownership is not the root cause of biased coverage. In contrast, the author contends, the media are more influenced by demographics than compa- ny ownership. If a medium serves a liberal community, it will more likely lean left, he states, and if it serves a conservative com- munity, it will more likely lean right. Media owners do not generally try to influence the public, the author maintains, because their goal is to maximize profit and satisfy the demands of the consumer. Mankiw is a pro- fessor of economics at Harvard University in Cambridge, Massachusetts.

AS YOU READ, CONSIDER THE FOLLOWING QUESTIONS:

1. According to the author, what are some phrases that are used more by Democrats than Republicans?

Consumers of the news, both from television and print, sometimes feel that they are getting not just the facts but also a sizable dose of ideological spin. Yet have you ever wondered about the root cause of the varying political slants of different media outlets?

That is precisely the question that a young economist, Matthew Gentzkow, has been asking. A professor at the Booth School of Business at the University of Chicago, Mr. Gentzkow was recently awarded the John Bates Clark Medal by the American Economic Association for the best economist under the age of 40. (Full disclosure: As one of the association's vice presidents, I was among those who voted to give him this award.) His main contributions have been to our understanding of the economics of the media industry.

One of his research articles, of which he was a co-author with Jesse Shapiro, a University of Chicago colleague, studied the political slant of more than 400 daily newspapers nationwide. The first step in their analysis, which was published in 2010, was simply to measure the slant of each paper. But that itself was no easy task.

Measuring Media Bias

When you listen to Sean Hannity of Fox News and Rachel Maddow of MSNBC, for example, you probably have no trouble figuring out who leans right and who leans left. But social scientists like Mr. Gentzkow and Mr. Shapiro need more than subjective impressions. They require objective measurement, especially when studying hundreds of news outlets. Here the authors were devilishly clever.

Mr. Gentzkow and Mr. Shapiro went to the Congressional Record and used a computer algorithm to find phrases that were particularly associated with the rhetoric of politicians of the two major political parties. They found that Democrats were more likely than Republicans to use phrases like "minimum wage," "oil and gas companies" and "wildlife refuge." Republicans more often referred to "tax relief," "pri-

One study concluded that the political slant of a newspaper is not determined by its ownership but by the community it serves. For example, the San Francisco Chronicle *is likely to lean left because it serves a liberal community.*

vate property rights" and "economic growth." While Democrats were more likely to mention Rosa Parks, Republicans were more likely to mention the Grand Ole Opry.

With specific phrases associated with political stands, the researchers then analyzed newspaper articles from 2005 to determine which papers leaned left and which leaned right. (They looked only at news articles and excluded opinion columns.) That is, they computed an objective, if imperfect, measure of political slant based on the choice of language.

To confirm the validity of their measure, Mr. Gentzkow and Mr. Shapiro showed that it was correlated with results from subjective surveys of readers. For example, both the computer algorithm and newspaper readers rated the *San Francisco Chronicle* as a distinctly liberal paper, and the *Washington Times* and the *Daily Oklahoman* as distinctly conservative ones. Both measures put the *New York Times* as moderately left of center and the *Wall Street Journal* as moderately right.

Percentage of Americans who say they prefer the source the most:

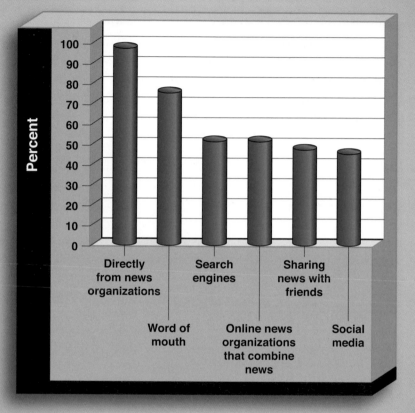

Taken from: American Press Institute, "How Americans Get Their News," March 17, 2014. www.americanpressinstitute.org.

With a measure of political slant in hand, the researchers then analyzed its determinants. That is, they examined why some papers write in a way that is more consistent with liberal rhetoric while others are more conservative.

Media Ownership Does Not Cause Bias

A natural hypothesis is that a media outlet's perspective reflects the ideology of its owner. Indeed, much regulatory policy is premised on precisely this view. Policy makers sometimes take a jaundiced view of media consolidation on the grounds that high levels of cross-ownership reduce the range of political perspectives available to consumers.

From their study of newspapers, however, Mr. Gentzkow and Mr. Shapiro, find little evidence to support this hypothesis. After accounting for confounding factors like geographic proximity, they find that two newspapers with the same owner are no more likely to be ideologically similar than two random papers. Moreover, they find no correlation between the political slant of a paper and the owner's ideology, as judged by political donations.

So, if not the owner's politics, what determines whether a newspaper leans left or right? To answer this question, Mr. Gentzkow and Mr. Shapiro focus on regional papers, ignoring the few with national scope, like the *Times*. They find that potential customers are crucial.

Demographics Play a Large Role in Media Bias

If a paper serves a liberal community, it is likely to lean left, and if it serves a conservative community, it is likely to lean right. In addition, once its political slant is set, a paper is more likely to be read by households who share its perspective.

Religiosity also plays a role in the story, and it helps Mr. Gentzkow and Mr. Shapiro sort out cause and effect. They find that in regions where a high percentage of the population attends church regularly, there are more conservatives, and newspapers have a conservative slant. They argue that because newspapers probably don't influence how religious a community is, the best explanation is that causation runs from the community's politics to the newspaper's slant, rather than the other way around.

The bottom line is simple: Media owners generally do not try to mold the population to their own brand of politics. Instead, like other business owners, they maximize profit by giving customers what they want.

These findings speak well of the marketplace. In the market for news, as in most other markets, Adam Smith's invisible hand leads producers to cater to consumers. But the findings also raise a more troubling question about the media's role as a democratic institution. How likely is it that we as citizens will change our minds, or reach compromise with those who have differing views, if all of us are getting our news from sources that reinforce the opinions we start with?

EVALUATING THE AUTHOR'S ARGUMENTS:

In this viewpoint, N. Gregory Mankiw argues that media ownership is not the root cause of biased news coverage. Who has the more convincing argument, in your opinion, Mankiw or Alison Langley, author of the previous viewpoint? Why?

Viewpoint

3

The Media Favor Democratic Party Policies

Michael Bargo Jr.

"That the national news media have a Democratic bias is well known."

In the following viewpoint, Michael Bargo Jr. argues that the media are liberally biased. He explores why the media have an intrinsic liberal bias, and he also examines how the media benefit from liberal leadership and policies. The media have a dependence on the Democratic Party, the author asserts, because it controls the largest US cities. In order to control the largest markets, the media must cooperate with the Democratic Party to advance both of their interests. As a result, Bargo states, the media have a financial interest to protect the policies of the Democratic Party. Bargo is a writer and photographer. In addition to his work in *American Thinker*, he is also the author of *Mexicago: How the Chicago Political Machine Created Sanctuary Policy to Exploit Immigrants and Grow Government*.

AS YOU READ, CONSIDER THE FOLLOWING QUESTIONS:

1. According to the author, what are the traditional explanations of why the media favor Democrats?

2. What is the media market, as stated by Bargo?
3. Who exposed the Illinois public sector pension debt, according to the author?

T he idea that the national news media have a Democratic bias is well known. The Media Research Center has found a clear difference between the way the national news media treat Democrats and Republicans. But the media effort is not just supportive of Democratic candidates and their policies and negative toward Republicans; it is also accompanied by a very aggressive effort to *defend* Democrats whenever the media reveal a scandal. These actions imply that the media has an agenda.

The nature and reasons for this agenda need to be investigated. An exploration of how and why media benefit from Democratic rule and policies may yield some useful insights. The traditional explanations of why the media favor Democrats are focused on their education: liberals are instructed in liberal ideology in college. The universities they

Reporters are held at bay by a staffer during a press conference in 2010 with Harry Reid, a Democratic senator from Nevada and the US Senate majority leader. Critics claim that the media protect the Democratic party for self-serving reasons.

attend also receive grant money to pursue research projects oriented to promote the liberal model of society, the economy, and environment.

Journalism students leave universities and enter the business world of television and print media as liberal reporters and writers. To understand how and why this liberal ideology operates in the huge national media business it's necessary to understand the nature of the traditional media business and its profit model. How media earn income, and the role the Democratic Party plays in their business model, is the crucial issue.

Demographics Factor into Media Bias

News media and political parties share one crucial characteristic: just as governments have geographic boundaries, news media outlets are bounded by their viewership or readership area, called their "media market." So they are naturally attracted to the largest media markets and wish to *preserve* them.

The crucial fact is that demographics are destiny for *both* media and political parties: both need people. And since the largest American cities are dominated by the Democratic Party, it follows that the media in these large cities must cooperate with the Democratic party to pursue their mutual agenda. Media then have a symbiotic dependence upon their host, the Democratic Party, or more accurately, the *Demographic* Party.

Of course this is not the only reason. Access to city hall is also important: if they anger the mayor with annoying questions they may lose their media credentials. And in Chicago, the Tribune Company, owners of the *Tribune* newspaper, benefited from state financial support. All of these issues, however, are sideshows to the main topic: demographics.

The media must also deal with the reality that since the largest cities are controlled by Democrats the majority of newspaper readers in these cities are Democrats. And

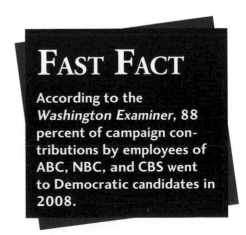

FAST FACT

According to the *Washington Examiner*, 88 percent of campaign contributions by employees of ABC, NBC, and CBS went to Democratic candidates in 2008.

media don't want to alienate their markets' voters. But it goes deeper than that.

While both the media and Democrats are intimately dependent on demographics for their survival *only the Democratic party controls* the populations of the major states and cities. And this has been true since at least 1930. As I have explained here before, the Party has aggressively acted to maintain their cities' populations.

Business Interests Influence Media Coverage

Most of the big cities' populations peaked in 1950 and have gradually fallen since. The media have not discussed these constant population losses. This is why the facts are not commonly known. But the facts are readily available from the Census Bureau. For example, the Census Bureau's Working Paper No. 76 gives a history of the populations of the largest American cities. Since Americans are always moving out of major cities to suburbs and other states (Chicago lost 180,000 black residents just from 2000 to 2010) cities need a constant flow of immigrants to replace them. But the flow of legal immigrants is far too small to replace the numbers of those who move out. Consequently the three biggest cities have adopted sanctuary policies for illegal immigration as their major strategy for preserving their populations.

The corollary is also true: cities without large illegal immigrant populations have lost the most residents. The list of American cities that have lost half their populations by 2000 includes not just Detroit, the best known case; but Pittsburgh, Cleveland, and St. Louis. Cities that have lost one-quarter to one-third and more of their populations include Boston, Baltimore, Cincinnati, Minneapolis, Newark, Philadelphia, Washington D.C. and Wilmington, DE. These are all in the Midwest and Northeast, the strongholds of liberal politics and journalism.

Illegal immigration requires not just the efforts of big city mayors but the willing cooperation of big city media outlets for it to exist and prosper. Illegal immigration is arguably the greatest, most far-reaching scheme of political corruption in history. To keep it functioning the media have been enthusiastic protectors of the Democratic politicians. Another reason the media have not criticized illegal immigration is that they are terrified that if their biggest markets shrink, their rev-

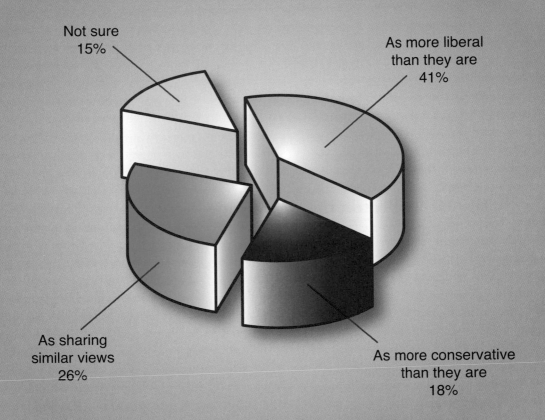

Not sure
15%

As more liberal
than they are
41%

As sharing
similar views
26%

As more conservative
than they are
18%

Taken from: Hasmussen Reports, "Only 6% Rate News Media as Very Trustworthy," February 28, 2013. www.rasmussenreports.com.

enues will shrink. And this fear, as they know better than anyone, is justified.

And this is the critically important fact: to pursue their demographic goals Democrats do not have to bribe the media with anything but their own business interest.

Democrats in the largest cities of L.A., Chicago, and New York sponsor illegal immigration in order to save public sector union jobs and congressional seats. But illegal immigrants are largely funded through federal programs. These program dollars create debt for all voters. Then the newspapers and TV news outlets in Chicago can't discuss the huge public debt, since it will make Democrats look bad, and hurt their own demographics. The Illinois public sector pension debt was exposed by the Illinois Better Government Association and Illinois Policy Institute. It was not researched by the big papers and TV stations. This debt continues to be grown by illegal immigration. So as the media ignore the great scheme of corruption they create more debt for the middle class and poor throughout the country. All because media want to protect their own "media market" turf and keep the population propped up.

The Media Protect the Democratic Party

So the implication is that because the media have their own financial interest rooted in demographics, they protect the corruption of the Democratic Party and cause the expansion of national debt and unemployment. These actions are a far cry from their self-proclaimed role of whistle-blowers and protectors of the people from government. Instead of exposing this corruption, they blame everything on corporate greed. One can ask whether liberal media focus on corporate greed to cover up their own advertising revenue greed and the government greed of the Democrats they support.

This is also why the media write numerous articles using and supporting the Democrats' rhetoric of helping the poor, taxing the rich, etc. They protect the "brand" of the Democrats since this rhetoric functions to expand federal programs, bring dollars into the biggest urban areas, and maintain the populations. They learned this rhetoric in liberal college classes. It prepared them for their job of advocating federal spending. It would be very difficult to find media stories that criticize these programs as being failures and exploiting the poor. This is further proof that they are willing participants in the preservation of Democratic control of their biggest markets.

EVALUATING THE AUTHOR'S ARGUMENTS:

In this viewpoint, Michael Bargo Jr. claims that the media favor the Democratic Party in order to protect media financial interests. Why might someone argue that it would be in the media's financial interests to maintain balanced rather than biased coverage?

Viewpoint

4

The Media Favor the Republicans' Policies

"The cozy relationship between Fox News Channel and top Republican presidential contenders . . . reeks of network-party incest."

Thomas F. Schaller

In the following viewpoint, Thomas F. Schaller argues that the media have more of a conservative slant than a liberal one. Media coverage on a few social issues does lean left, the author contends, but on a structural level, the bias of the media is conservative. He attributes this to conservative think tanks, which influence newspaper opinion content and are better funded than liberal think tanks. In addition, the author states, syndicated conservative columnists dominate opinion pages throughout the United States. The US profit-oriented media structure benefits conservatives, the author asserts, yet conservatives continue to argue that liberals have an advantage in the media. Schaller teaches political science at the University of Maryland, Baltimore County.

AS YOU READ, CONSIDER THE FOLLOWING QUESTIONS:

1. According to the author, what issues generally have a conservative bias in the media?

2. Why are positive portrayals of gay Americans in the news not evidence of media bias, as stated by Schaller?
3. According to the author, which Republican presidential candidates have worked for Fox News?

L iberal media bias.

So incessant is this complaint from conservatives that the three words string together as one, like Holy Roman Empire. But like the old saw about that infamous regime being neither holy nor Roman nor an empire, liberal media bias is largely a misnomer.

Yes: The opinion media generally skew liberal on social issues related to abortion, gay rights, religion and maybe—maybe—guns. But that's about the extent of it.

On issues of war and peace, taxes and spending and government regulation, the corporate-owned American media are frequently anything but liberal. Of course, avowedly liberal confines such as *The*

"Next...an in-depth report on corporate corruption - excluding, of course, our parent company."

Nation or the *American Prospect* magazines, left-wing blogs, or the superb MSNBC weekend shows hosted by Chris Hayes and Melissa Harris-Perry regularly feature reports or commentaries about American poverty, homelessness, economic inequality, prison conditions, child welfare or domestic violence. But across the nation, mainstream coverage of such issues tends to be spotty.

Why? Because producers know Americans don't want to have to think about reportage on these national problems. Sordid stories about the Kardashians sell magazines and draw eyes and ears to radio, TV and the Internet far better than do sordid tales of bereft orphans.

Take the supposed problem of political correctness in the media, yet another red (or Red America) herring. The positive portrayals of gay Americans in the news—or in movies, television shows like *Modern Family* or the clever new Kindle ad where a gay man and a straight woman both mention their husbands—aren't evidence of a politically correct bias. They're evidence of profit-correctness by publishers and producers who know gay Americans are consumers, too.

Conservative Media Bias Is Real

As [journalist] Eric Alterman has demonstrated in his book *What Liberal Media?* conservative think tanks, which are responsible for much newspaper opinion content, are far better funded than their liberal counterparts. Anyone who thinks the interests of corporate America are muted in our media needs a reality check.

Meanwhile, we almost never hear about conservative media bias. It's very real.

Last week [March 1, 2013] came news of a pack of conservative pundits, led by [conservative commentator] Joshua Treviño and including writers for *Commentary* magazine and the *Red State* blog,

In 2010 Media Matters for America published an article on the conservative media bias they believe is shown by Fox News.

who took nearly $400,000 to advocate on behalf of the government of Malaysia. Keep this in mind next time any of these foreign government water-carriers say liberals are insufficiently patriotic. (At least in the case of the conservative columnist Armstrong Williams, the sources for the payola he took during George W. Bush's presidency to write favorable columns about national education policy were domestic.)

And how about the cozy relationship between Fox News Channel and top Republican presidential contenders? In recent years, Newt Gingrich, Mike Huckabee, Sarah Palin and Rick Santorum have all been on Fox's revolving-door payroll. There's nothing illegal or even unethical about this, but it reeks of network-party incest.

Syndicated conservative columnists dominate op-ed pages nation-wide. A few years ago, Media Matters for America [MMFA] conducted a survey of American daily papers. MMFA found that 60 percent of papers ran more conservative columnists than liberal columnists and 20 percent ran more liberals than conservatives, with the remaining 20 percent split.

The Media Structure Benefits Conservatives

Question: If the U.S. media are so bad, what sort of alternative might conservatives prefer?

I presume no self-respecting, First Amendment–revering American of any ideological stripe wants a state-run or state-censored media like those I've seen up close in China, Saudi Arabia and Zimbabwe. If conservative fury with National Public Radio is any indication, a state-funded but independent media like the Canadian Broadcasting Corporation or the British Broadcasting Corporation would be nearly as unacceptable.

The truth is that the ideal media structure for conservatives is one in which large, profit-oriented and politically powerful corporations own the broadcast and cable television networks, the major newspapers (the *Wall Street Journal* boasts the nation's largest circulation) and newspaper chains, and broadcast radio. And that's exactly what we have in America.

Yet the "liberal media bias" complaint persists. Conspiracy-minded conservatives should ask themselves: If liberals really owned and ran the media, why isn't "conservative media bias" the more common term in national politics?

EVALUATING THE AUTHOR'S ARGUMENTS:

In this viewpoint, Thomas F. Schaller claims that the media have a conservative bias and favor Republican policies. Who, in your opinion, has the more convincing argument, Schaller or Michael Bargo Jr., author of the previous viewpoint? Why?

Media Bias Portrays Muslims as Violent

Sarah Kendzior

"The Western media reinforce the very stereotype of a united, violent 'Muslim world.'"

In the following viewpoint, Sarah Kendzior argues that the Western media have an anti-Muslim bias. The media routinely use the phrase *the Muslim world*, the author asserts, and they associate Muslims with violence. Yet using this phrase leads to inaccurate reporting, Kendzior maintains, because it lumps together more than a billion and a half people across the world into a homogeneous group. Instead of making generalizations about Muslims, the author contends, the media should focus on dictatorship and factionalism, which have been as essential in shaping politics in Muslim-majority regions. Kendzior is an anthropologist and writer on politics, economy, and media.

AS YOU READ, CONSIDER THE FOLLOWING QUESTIONS:

1. According to the author, how is Islam often presented in Western media?
2. As stated by the author, how many hits result from googling *Christian world* and how many from *Muslim world*?

3. What is the harmful impact of the media viewing the Muslim world as a problem, according to the author?

On September 12, [2012] the day after the attacks on the US diplomatic missions in Egypt and Libya, the *New York Times* set out to explain what it called the "anguished relationship between the United States and the Muslim world". According to the *Times*, the "Muslim world" was prone to outbursts of violence, and the reaction to the 14-minute anti-Islam movie trailer *The Innocence of Muslims* was both baffling and predictable. "Once again, Muslims were furious," wrote reporter Robert F. Worth, "and many in the West found themselves asking why Islam seems to routinely answer such desecrations with violence."

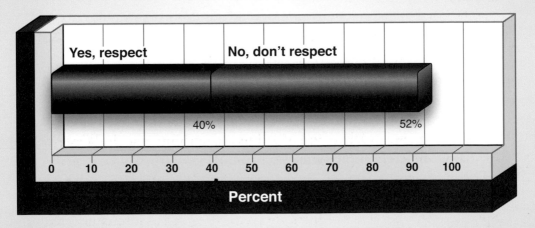

Americans Believe Western Societies Do Not Respect Muslim Societies

Do you believe Western societies respect Muslim societies, or do you believe Western societies do not respect Muslim societies?

Yes, respect — 40%

No, don't respect — 52%

Percent

Taken from: Gallup, "Islamophobia: Understanding Anti-Muslim Sentiment in the West," 2011. www.gallup.com.

Other media outlets echoed the claim that "the Muslim world" was consumed by anger, and had long been so. The Associated Press offered a look back at "Five other incidents that inspired rage in the Muslim world", crediting over a billion people for the actions of a few thousand in their search for historical continuity. Others took a psychoanalytic approach. "Why is the Muslim world so easily offended?" asked *Washington Post* columnist Fouad Ajami. "Madness in the Muslim World: Help Me Understand," pleaded a blogger for the *Houston Chronicle.*

It is time to retire the phrase "the Muslim world" from the Western media. Using the phrase in the manner above disregards not only history and politics, but accurate reporting of contemporary events. The protests that took place around the world ranged in scale and intensity, in the participants' willingness to use violence, and in their rationales. The majority of the "Muslim world" did not participate in these protests, nor did all of the Muslims who protested the video advocate the bloodshed that took place in Libya.

By reducing a complex set of causes and conflicts to the rage of an amorphous mass, the Western

> # FAST FACT
>
> Wired.co.uk reported in 2012 that the majority of organizations that sought to shape public opinion about Islam after September 11, 2001, delivered pro-Muslim messages, but the US media focused on the messages of fringe organizations that pandered to fear and anger.

media reinforce the very stereotype of a united, violent "Muslim world" that both the makers of the anti-Islam video and the Islamist instigators of the violence perpetuate.

Misleading Generalizations About Islam

Essentialist views of Islam and Muslims are nothing new. In Western media, Islam is often presented as a contagion, with Muslims as the afflicted, helpless to their own hostile impulses. What is different about the current crisis is that it comes in the aftermath of the "Arab Spring"—another series of intricate events depicted as interconnected and inevitable. Democracy would "spread" from one Muslim country to another, analysts argued, regardless of the unique historical trajectories of individual states. Some analysts went so far as to suggest it would spread to Central Asia, a region of largely isolationist dictatorships uninfluenced by Middle Eastern politics. The current protests are being portrayed as an "Arab Winter"—a simplistic reversal of a simplistic perception of success, with Muslims, undifferentiated, receiving the blame.

There is, of course, cohesion among Muslims, in the sense that there is cohesion among followers of any faith. The notion of the *ummah* [community] is an essential part of Islamic doctrine. But the way the idea of "the Muslim world" is expressed within Islamic communities is different from the way it is expressed outside them. It is rare to hear the phrase "the Christian world" used in the English-language media, because doing so would generalise about the motives of over 2 billion

A sign on the main entrance of the US consulate in Benghazi, Libya, expresses disapproval of the attack on the building by a small group of Muslims. Many feel that the Western media clumps all Muslims together, unfairly stereotyping more than 1 billion people.

people. No such respect applies to the world's 1.5 billion Muslims. Googling the phrase "the Christian world" yields 5.8 million results, while the phrase "the Muslim world" gives over 87 million results, many of them wondering what is "wrong" with the queried target. When the phrase "the Muslim world" is invoked, it is usually to reduce, denigrate or impugn.

The Western media's broad-stroke regionalism means that conflicts within individual Muslim-majority states become marginalised. Syrians posting on Twitter wondered how the world could give so much attention to a conflict that killed seven people while dozens of Syrians are killed by state security forces every day—documenting, as one commenter noted, their own demise in videos that receive far less attention than the bigoted pseudo-cinema of one American. Similarly, the violence at the diplomatic missions in Cairo and Benghazi was initially conflated, with "Muslim rage" being presented as a root cause for two distinct conflicts. The tendency to see "the Muslim world" as a problem in general means that specific problems within Muslim countries go unseen.

Dispelling Stereotypes

Soon after the destruction of the US embassy in Benghazi and the deaths of four Americans, a protest was held against the men who murdered them. Libyan citizens held English-language signs declaring "Benghazi is against terrorism" and "Sorry Americans this is not the behavior of our Islam and Profit [sic]". Photos of the protest, distributed by Libya Alhurra Livestream, went viral on Facebook and Twitter.

The Libyans protesting were aware that not only Libyans, but Muslims in general, would be blamed for the violence that took place, because the small group of Muslims who stormed the embassy would be seen as representative of all. They gave the rare apology that Western commentators often encourage Muslims to make on behalf of others who commit violence in the name of Islam. But while the sentiment of the protestors is appreciated by many Americans—and the photos likely assuaged some prejudices—such explanations should not be necessary. Ordinary people should not be assumed to share the beliefs of violent criminals who share their faith.

The Innocence of Muslims was made by Nakoula Basseley Nakoula, an Egyptian-American who hates Muslims. It was found on YouTube and put on Egyptian television by Sheikh Khaled Abdullah, a man trying to convince the world that Americans hate Muslims. This was a perfect storm of gross and deceitful parties depicting each other in the most vile terms, and then living up to each others' worst expectations.

The answer to such invective is not to reinforce it through media portrayals of "Muslims" as a collective. The media should instead pay more attention to individual states, conflicts and leaders, since dictatorship and factionalism have been as essential in shaping politics in Muslim-majority regions as has religion. The current crisis demonstrates how corrupt parties use religion as an incitement to violence and a means to political gain. The Western media should not play party to their prejudices.

EVALUATING THE AUTHOR'S ARGUMENTS:

In this viewpoint, Sarah Kendzior asserts that the Western media have an anti-Muslim bias. Do you agree with her argument that the use of the term "Muslim world" presents a biased portrayal of Islam? Why or why not?

Media Bias Portrays Muslims as Peace Loving

William Kilpatrick

"The media is by and large committed to the narrative that Islam is a religion of peace."

In the following viewpoint, William Kilpatrick argues that the media have created a pro-Islamic narrative. In an attempt to portray Islam as a religion of peace, Kilpatrick asserts, the media either underreport incidents of Islamic terrorism or shape the coverage to show that the violence is not linked to Islam. As a result, the author says, the mainstream media have covered up the true extent of Islamic violence worldwide. Whether intentionally or not, the mainstream media in the United States have taken Islam's side in the information war, the author maintains. Kilpatrick has written for *Catholic World Report*, *National Catholic Register*, *Saint Austin Review*, *Investor's Business Daily*, and *FrontPage Magazine*. He is also the author of several books about cultural and religious issues, including *Psychological Seduction; Why Johnny Can't Tell Right from Wrong;* and *Christianity, Islam and Atheism: The Struggle for the Soul of the West.*

AS YOU READ, CONSIDER THE FOLLOWING QUESTIONS:
1. Who is responsible for most press censorship in the United States, according to the author?
2. As stated by Kilpatrick, Muslim jihadists injured how many people in a Chinese train station in 2014?
3. What event received more media coverage than the Fort Hood shooter trial, according to the author?

A ccording to Reporters Without Borders, the U.S. has dropped to 46th place in press freedom. The lowered ranking was based on the conviction of the WikiLeaks informant, the effort to punish NSA [National Security Agency] leaker Edward Snowden, and the Justice Department's monitoring of reporters.

Unmentioned by the report, however, is an equally serious cause for concern. Most press censorship in the U.S. is self-imposed. The masters of the media are quite willing to suppress certain news stories without any government encouragement. This can be accomplished in several ways: by not reporting a story, by providing only minimal coverage, or by shaping the story to fit a pre-existing narrative. There may be "eight million stories in the naked city," as the old television series informed us, but the news producers are the ones who decide which stories you will hear and what slant they will be given.

> **FAST FACT**
>
> According to the American Press Institute, 76 percent of Americans reported getting news on a daily basis in 2014, whether by watching, reading, or listening to it.

The Media Portray Islam as a Peaceful Religion

Take the matter of Islamic terrorism. The media is by and large committed to the narrative that Islam is a religion of peace. Hence, they tend to underreport incidents of Islamic terrorism or else they shape the story to fit the narrative that violence has nothing to do with Islam. For example, did you know that the group of knife-wielding assailants who slashed to death 29 people and injured 140 at a crowded Chinese train station on March 1, 2014 were Muslim jihadists? The fact that the killers were Muslims is carried in some reports, usually at the end of the story, but the main impression given by most of the reporting is that they were "separatists" who were making a "political" statement about "repression" of ethnic minorities. The words "jihad" or "jihadists" are notable by their absence from most reports.

Did you know that Michael Adebolajo, and Michael Adebowale, the murderers of British soldier Lee Rigby [on May 22, 2013] have Muslim names? After their conversion to Islam they took the names Mujaahid Abu Hamza and Ismail bin Abdullah, respectively. In this case and in others, however, the mainstream media refrained from using the Muslim names. After the killing, Abu Hamza forced a passerby to video record his message to the public. While several TV stations carried the message, most of them cut out the part where he referred to passages from the Qur'an as justification for his act. Also unreported was the fact that Abu Hamza handed a blood-stained note full of Qur'an quotations to a bystander. Almost all news reports, however, did manage to give a lot of space to Prime Minister David Cameron's assurance that the killing had nothing to do with Islam. . . .

Supporters of Tarek Mehanna rally outside the federal courthouse in Boston in 2012. The case may have received little US media attention because of the negative association with Islam.

Many Stories of Islamic Violence Are Unreported

The above are cases in which the media chose to slant the news by leaving out key details which might connect Islamic beliefs to terrorism. . . . Just as significant, however, are the stories that go unreported or underreported. It is not unfair to say that by giving the silent treatment to the vast majority of incidents, the mainstream media has managed to effectively cover up the sheer magnitude of Islamic violence worldwide. The streaming headlines at the bottom of your TV screen that detail the daily toll taken by jihadists represent only a fraction of the actual occurrences. . . .

All of the following stories were covered to some extent by the media but not to the extent that they were likely to stick in the memory for long. It is very unlikely, for example, that you would recall the case of Nuradin Abdi, who was sentenced in 2007 to 10 years in prison for a planned jihad attack against an Ohio mall. Nor is it likely that you would remember the case of Derrick Shareef, who was sentenced in 2008 to 35 years in prison for plotting to explode grenades at a Rockford, Illinois shopping mall. A convert to Islam, Shareef was recorded as saying that he wanted to kill infidels. How about Tarek Mehanna? In 2009, the 27-year-old Massachusetts man was charged with conspiring to attack shoppers in U.S. malls. According to the complaint, Mehanna and his co-conspirators often discussed their desire to participate in "violent jihad against American interests."

While it's unlikely you will have a good memory of these trials, it's very likely you will not have forgotten the George Zimmerman–Trayvon Martin case [in which Zimmerman fatally shot seventeen-year-old Martin in 2012]. That shooting might have remained a local news affair, but influential people in and outside the media decided to turn it into a major national story. Am I suggesting a conscious and deliberate suppression of some stories and a conscious inflation of others? Yes and no. In some cases, yes, the bias is quite deliberate. But many cases of lopsided reporting can probably be attributed to an automatic response. Some cases will seem more important to the news editors because they fit into a preconceived narrative, and other cases will receive less attention because they don't fit the established narratives. Indeed, if some cases were to be explored in depth, they might challenge and even explode the narrative. Hence, there is much less incentive to dig into such stories. The trial of Major Nidal Hasan, the

Most Americans Say They Know Little About Islam

How much do you know about the Muslim religion?

	Nov 2001	Mar 2002	Jul 2003	Jul 2005	Aug 2007	Aug 2010
A great deal	6%	5%	4%	5%	7%	9%
Some	32%	29%	27%	28%	34%	35%
Not very much	37%	37%	39%	36%	33%	30%
Nothing at all	24%	28%	29%	30%	25%	25%
Don't know	1%	1%	1%	1%	1%	—

Taken from: Pew Research Center for the People and the Press and Pew Forum on Religion and Public Life, "Public Remains Conflicted over Islam," August 24, 2010. www.pewforum.com.

Fort Hood [US Army post in Texas] shooter, was at least as significant an event as the trial of George Zimmerman and it took place, moreover, in roughly the same time frame. Yet it received nowhere near the coverage of the other trial. The media was quite happy to focus on the supposedly racist motivations of Zimmerman but quite reluctant to look into the blatant jihadist motivations of Major Hasan. . . .

The Media Misinform Citizens About Islam

While the mainstream media can't very well ignore a plot to blow up a major U.S. to Canada train line, they can minimize the coverage, and they can and do downplay the Islamic connection.

The average Western citizen can be forgiven if he is not up-to-speed on the numerous successful and attempted jihad attacks in the U.S., Canada, and Europe. There is abundant evidence that the opinion-makers don't want us to think too much about the subject. When an attack occurs or when one is foiled, the media give it a perfunctory nod and then almost immediately lose interest in the story. Are they hoping that we will lose interest too?

As political scientist Samuel Huntington observed, we are in a civilizational struggle with Islam. One of the major fronts in that conflict is the information war, and thus far Islam seems to be winning it hands-down. Why? Because the Western media has adopted as its own Islam's narrative about itself—that it is a religion of peace that has been hijacked by a handful of misunderstanders. The result is that what information we get about Islam is filtered through a rose-colored prism. Whether consciously or through force of habit, the mainstream media has effectively taken Islam's side in the information war. Thanks to the media's pandering, Western citizens are ill-informed about Islam, and as a result they are unprepared for the more aggressive forms of jihad to which the information jihad is merely a prelude.

EVALUATING THE AUTHOR'S ARGUMENTS:

In this viewpoint, William Kilpatrick claims that the news media censor coverage of terrorist attacks committed by Muslims in order to portray Islam as a peaceful religion. Who has the more convincing argument, Kilpatrick or the author of the previous viewpoint? Explain your answer, citing a piece of evidence or quote that had an impact on your opinion.

Media Bias Hurts Transgender Persons

Jos Truitt

"By spreading the same tired stereotypes about trans people, too many in the media are instead contributing directly to . . . discrimination and violence."

In the following viewpoint, Jos Truitt argues that the media are biased against members of the transgender community. The media have routinely created factually inaccurate stories that dehumanize the lives of transgender people, the author maintains. This negative coverage has contributed to discrimination and violence against members of the transgender community. Members of the transgender community are battling an industry that fails to see them as human beings, the author avers. The identities of transgender people are valid, Truitt contends, and questioning or ignoring their existence is not legitimate journalism. Truitt is a writer, printmaker, and executive director of Feministing.com. She writes, speaks, and trains on topics such as transgender issues, abortion access, and media representation.

AS YOU READ, CONSIDER THE FOLLOWING QUESTIONS:
1. Which mainstream publication featured a transgender TV star on its cover in 2014, according to the author?
2. As stated by Truitt, what happened after the *Chicago Sun-Times* republished an article stating that transgender identities are invalid?
3. According to the author, what are some consequences of the media's negative coverage of the transgender community?

For too long, the media has published irresponsible, factually inaccurate and dehumanizing articles on transgender women. For many years, trans people appeared in print almost exclusively as dead bodies—almost always of murdered trans women of color, who face the highest rates of violence in the LGBT [lesbian, gay, bisexual, and transgender] community.

Articles regularly use the wrong name and gender pronouns for these murder victims, and paint salacious pictures that suggest these women were sex workers who likely tricked men into sleeping with them and ultimately "had it coming".

Fighting Negative Press Coverage

The trans community has fought to end this negative press coverage—and for the media to actually write about the real lives and struggles of trans people. For too long.

Then, last week [May 28, 2014], *Time* published a cover story titled "The Transgender Tipping Point", featuring *Orange Is the New Black* star Laverne Cox and offering a broad introduction to transgender issues for the magazine's readers. Many trans advocates, including myself, think the article is imperfect—but it's also the best example of a positive, educational article on trans people and issues in such a high profile space.

So of course Kevin D. Williamson at the conservative *National Review* felt it necessary to respond to this important moment in mainstream education by publishing an op-ed calling Laverne Cox "an effigy of a woman", referring to her with male pronouns, and claiming —in the face of scientific and medical consensus—that biological facts "prove" that transgender identities are invalid. Williamson also published a follow-up piece digging in his heels when his op-ed received the expected (and well-deserved) backlash.

That Williamson and the *National Review* would publish this click-bait hate speech is sadly no surprise. Then came an unexpected and considerably more disturbing turn: the *Chicago Sun-Times* chose to republish the op-ed over the weekend—and keep it up on their site

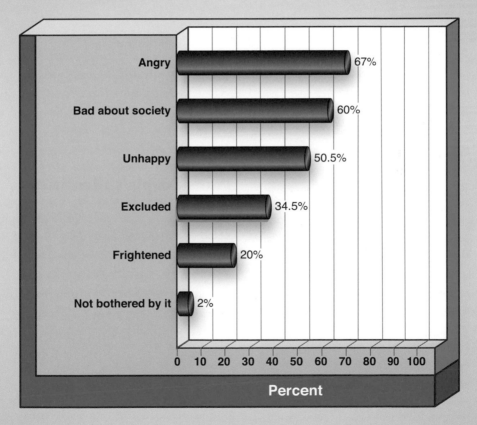

Transgender People's Reactions to Media Portrayals

Percentage of respondents who said negative items about trans people made them feel...

Angry — 67%
Bad about society — 60%
Unhappy — 50.5%
Excluded — 34.5%
Frightened — 20%
Not bothered by it — 2%

Percent

Note: Total respondents = 232.

Taken from: Trans Media Watch, "How Transgender People Experience the Media," April 2010. www.transmediawatch.org.

until it was pulled on Tuesday [June 3, 2014,] after immense pressure from advocates, the trans community and other media organizations.

The paper released the following statement:

> We try to present a range of views on an issue, not only those views we may agree with, but also those we don't agree with. A recent op-ed piece we ran online that was produced by another publication initially struck as provocative. Upon further consideration, we concluded the essay did not include some key facts and its overall tone was not consistent with what we seek to publish. The column failed to acknowledge that the American Medical Association and the American Psychological Association have deemed transgender-related care medically necessary for transgender people. It failed as well to acknowledge the real and undeniable pain and discrimination felt by transgender people, who suffer from notably higher rates of depression and suicide. We have taken the post down and we apologize for the oversight.

(Williamson, of course, wrote a second follow-up Tuesday night, decrying the *Sun-Times*'s decision as "an unhappy reminder that postoperative transsexuals are not the only men who have had their characteristic equipment removed".)

Trans People's Identities Are Valid

While I'm glad the *Sun-Times* took down the article and released an apology, we never should have had to fight their publication of this op-ed. The paper's apology is particularly infuriating, as it implies that a range of viewpoints on *the validity of trans people's existence* are worthy of publication. While the editors acknowledge that the medical establishment considers trans healthcare medically necessary, and that we face extreme discrimination and violence, the

Transgender actress Laverne Cox (left) and Delores Nettles, mother of slain transgender woman Islan Nettles, attend the 2014 New York City Pride March.

Sun-Times fails to make a clear statement that trans people's identities are valid and that questioning this is not legitimate journalism.

It's not like this is the first time someone has had to correct journalists on these topics.

Only last year [2013], when WikiLeaks whistle-blower Chelsea Manning came out as a trans woman, major media organizations ignored their own style guides, misgendered Manning, questioned her gender and ultimately made "the story" about the difficulties of reporting on trans people—despite the fact that most of them already had guidelines in place on how to do so respectfully. (Williamson published a hit piece on Manning at the *National Review* at that time that is very similar to his piece about Cox—questioning the legitimacy of trans women's identities is quite a pastime of his.)

In January [2014], the website Grantland (which is owned by ESPN Internet Ventures, a subsidiary of the Walt Disney Company) published an article—ostensibly about the inventor of a golf putter—that resulted in a prurient quest to uncover the subject's trans status, and which may have contributed to the article's subject's suicide.

Even incredible public representatives of the trans community like Laverne Cox and Janet Mock have been asked salacious questions about their genitals and transitions by journalists who seem more interested in talking about the particulars of our bodies than about our lives.

Each time the media fails so massively in reporting on trans people, advocates remind them that they already have style guides in place, and that organizations like GLAAD [Gay and Lesbian Alliance Against Defamation] provide glossaries that can easily give them the basics on trans issues. Yet time and again we see the same failures in the press, because far too many people in positions of power in media refuse to accept the existence of trans people and apparently think that, as journalists, they get to decide if our identities are valid or not.

The Media Contribute to Discrimination Against Trans People

Despite the positive publicity generated by Cox's *Time* cover, trans women are still fighting for others in media to recognize our basic humanity. And there are very real consequences of this terrible media coverage: the trans community, particularly low-income trans women and trans people of color, face astronomically high rates of discrimination in housing, employment and public accommodations; are far too often homeless or incarcerated; and trans women of color are facing a global epidemic of violence.

Publications could, in fact, fill their pages or websites with articles about the very real issues faced by trans people—and the work many of us are doing to end the injustices we all face. For instance, currently, a 16-year-old trans girl of color has been locked up in an adult prison for over 50 days without charges after already suffering abuse at the hands of the Connecticut Department of Children and Families—a gross case of abuse at the hands of the state. That story is undoubtedly more deserving of space in a publication than Williamson's stale, factually inaccurate rant.

The media has a responsibility to report on the world in a way that informs. But by spreading the same tired stereotypes about trans people, too many in the media are instead contributing directly to the kind of ignorance and dehumanization that breeds this discrimination and violence. Editors, columnists and reporters need to stop wasting space questioning trans people's right to exist. We're here, we're living, and we deserve to have our humanity recognized and represented.

EVALUATING THE AUTHOR'S ARGUMENTS:

In this viewpoint, Jos Truitt contends that the media's stereotypical portrayal of the transgender community has contributed to violence and discrimination against transgender people. Do you think positive media coverage would reduce discrimination against people in the transgender community? Explain your answer.

Viewpoint 8

Media Bias Promotes Gay Marriage

Cliff Kincaid

"Media bias is . . . evident in the fact that 13 of the top 15 newspapers in the country have editorialized their support for homosexual marriage."

In the following viewpoint, Cliff Kincaid argues that the media have embarked on a pro-gay campaign in order to normalize homosexuality. Kincaid highlights the power of organizations such as the National Lesbian and Gay Journalists Association in the coverage of the homosexual marriage debate. The author asserts that the media provide slanted coverage of homosexuality in order to increase acceptance of the gay lifestyle. Kincaid states that the power of the media has changed the political landscape for the benefit of the homosexual movement in the United States. Kincaid is the director of Accuracy in Media's Center for Investigative Journalism.

AS YOU READ, CONSIDER THE FOLLOWING QUESTIONS:
1. According to the author, the media failed to cover what event in Washington, DC?
2. What message would homosexual activists like to keep out of the media, as stated by the author?
3. According to Kincaid, how much money has the founder of Quark, Inc. donated to the gay rights movement?

Offending the moral sensibilities of millions of Americans, *Time* Magazine is featuring cover stories [in March 2013] showing two white homosexual couples kissing. The *Right Scoop* blog ran a "censored version of the offensive covers."

John Aravosis, the homosexual activist who runs Americablog.com, said this is part of a propaganda campaign to normalize homosexuality. He said, "The kiss has been quite a powerful political weapon in the gay arsenal for a while now. And checking our archives, it's rather amazing how important the 'gay kiss' has been to our political struggle over the years."

The Media Are Normalizing Homosexuality

The purpose is to desensitize people to homosexuality and increase acceptance of the lifestyle.

Media bias is also evident in the influence of the media-funded National Lesbian & Gay Journalists Association (NLGJA).

The NLGJA says coverage of the homosexual marriage debate before the Supreme Court was "balanced—supportive even," and that program hosts "felt compelled to disagree with them [opponents of homosexual marriage] on air."

We noted the media's failure to cover the March for Marriage in Washington, D.C.

On the *Time* cover photos, the NLGJA said, "The black-and-white photos are an interesting, provocative selection. The magazine didn't opt for family photos of smiling, nonthreatening gay and lesbian families and their kids: It went for the part of same-sex marriage that may be most off-putting to mainstream cultures. The kissing, the sexuality. It's a bold choice for a mainstream publication to make."

> **FAST FACT**
>
> Between 1996 and 2014, the percentage of the US population in favor of same-sex marriage increased from 27 to 54 percent.

Regarding the story itself, the NLGJA said it "was largely positive, save for a colorful sentence about AIDS and bathhouses."

The offensive phrase was that the deadly disease AIDS was "burning outward from the bathhouses. . . ." These are places where anonymous

ABC News reporter Amy Robach addresses the audience at a 2014 National Lesbian and Gay Journalists Association (NLGJA) event. Some critics contend that the NLGJA is highly influential in media coverage of pro-gay stories.

gay sex is common. Homosexuals are determined to keep coverage of the health hazards of homosexuality out of mainstream media.

On his *Reliable Sources* program, supposedly devoted to media criticism, host Howard Kurtz featured two homosexual rights supporters, John Aravosis and Jennifer Rubin, who writes the *Right Turn* blog for the *Washington Post*.

Nevertheless, he noted the bias in the coverage, explaining that "Liberal commentators are thrilled that the marriage debate is swinging their way, at least in the court of public opinion, while many conservative pundits were muted or surprisingly supportive." He cited Bill O'Reilly of Fox News declaring that "The compelling argument is on the side of homosexuals," and dismissing opponents as Bible-thumpers.

The latter was apparently a reference to the Christian teaching that marriage involves a man and a woman and that homosexuality is prohibited in the Bible because it is unnatural and sinful.

Rush Limbaugh countered: "So how many of you who watch Fox are Bible thumpers? Do you think there are any Bible thumpers, quote/unquote, that watch Fox? Because last night you were sort of marginalized on *The [O'Reilly] Factor* as not having a compelling argument and just being a bunch of Bible thumpers."

Changing the Political Landscape

Limbaugh also noted the influence of the "Gay Mafia," which he described as "the activist homosexual lobby" contributing "big bucks" to the Democratic Party, and leading the campaign for homosexual marriage.

Interestingly, it was *Time* Magazine which ran a 2008 story, "The Gay Mafia That's Redefining Liberal Politics." One of the rich members of the group was identified as Timothy Gill of Denver, the founder of Quark, Inc., a computer software company, and a tech multimillionaire, who says he has singlehandedly "invested more than $220 million" in the cause of homosexual rights through his Gill Foundation.

An earlier 2007 *Time* story, "The Gay Mogul Changing U.S. Politics," estimated his fortune at $425 million. Denver political analyst Floyd Ciruli compared Gill to George Soros: "What you have are extremely wealthy individuals who aren't personally interested in running for anything but have this tremendous passion. Like George Soros, Tim Gill is actually changing the political landscape."

But Soros, too, has a big hand in changing the landscape for the benefit of the homosexuals. In 2009 he financed the "New Beginning Initiative" to encourage the [Barack] Obama administration to make "policy changes" to benefit the homosexual movement.

The Gill Foundation is also behind "OutGiving," which claims to have "provided unique opportunities for lesbian, gay, bisexual,

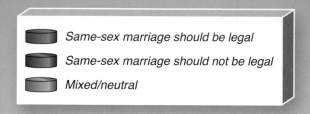

Opinions of the News Media and the General Public About Same-Sex Marriage

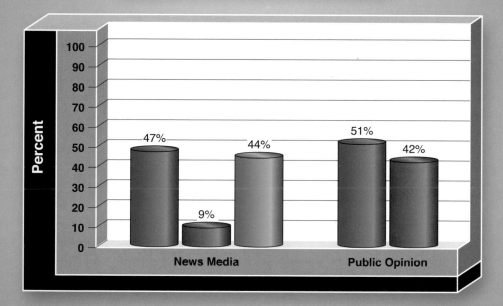

- Same-sex marriage should be legal
- Same-sex marriage should not be legal
- Mixed/neutral

News Media: 47%, 9%, 44%
Public Opinion: 51%, 42%

(Percent — vertical axis 0 to 100)

Note: Numbers for news media represent percent of stories with statements supporting or opposing gay marriage for the period from March 18 to May 12, 2013. Public opinion numbers represent percent of respondents; mixed/neutral was not an option for the public opinion surveys.

Taken from: Paul Hitlin, Mark Jukowitz, and Amy Mitchell, "News Coverage Conveys Strong Momentum for Same-Sex Marriage," Pew Research Center, June 17, 2013. www.journalism.org.

transgender (LGBT), and allied donors to gather in a private setting to engage in conversation with each other and with respected LGBT and allied leaders about ways to advance equality through philanthropy." OutGiving says it has "inspired hundreds of donors to give more strategically and more generously to improve the lives of LGBT people across the country and around the world."

The biannual OutGiving Conference is said to be "geared toward individuals whose annual philanthropy exceeds $25,000 and who are interested in increasing the effectiveness of their giving in support of the LGBT movement."

They are meeting in Chicago, Illinois this week [April 1, 2013]. However, the event is by "invitation-only," and "private," and "no media are permitted."

Don't look for the homosexuals in the media to blow their cover.

The Media Support Gay Marriage

Media bias is also evident in the fact that 13 of the top 15 newspapers in the country have editorialized their support for homosexual marriage. The pro-homosexual American Foundation for Equal Rights identified these publications as:

- *USA Today*
- The *New York Times*
- *Los Angeles Times*
- *San Jose Mercury News*
- The *Washington Post*
- *Daily News*
- *Chicago Tribune*
- *Chicago Sun-Times*
- The *Dallas Morning News*
- *Houston Chronicle*
- The *Philadelphia Inquirer*
- The *Arizona Republic*
- The *Denver Post*

The homosexual movement senses victory is just around the corner. And Limbaugh himself says federal approval of homosexual marriage may be "inevitable." But referring to the group's March 26 [2013] March for Marriage, Brian Brown of the National Organization for Marriage said, "Forget the media hype and confusion, our numbers today show that the American people are strongly pro-marriage and pro-marriage Americans aren't going anywhere. This is the beginning of the fight to protect marriage. Our opponents know this, which is why they are hoping the Supreme Court will cut short a debate they know they will ultimately lose if the political process and democracy are allowed to run their course. Those who believe that marriage is the unique and special union of one man and one woman are on the right side of history."

EVALUATING THE AUTHOR'S ARGUMENTS:

In this viewpoint, Cliff Kincaid claims that the media have a pro-gay rights agenda. Why might someone argue that the media have a bias against members of the gay community?

Chapter 3

What Are the Best Ways to Fight Media Bias?

Being informed about reliable news sources, understanding bias in the media, and limiting exposure to too much news can all help consumers to reduce the role that bias plays in their news consumption.

Media Literacy Helps Consumers Fight Media Bias

"Reading, watching, and listening with a critical eye and an engaged mind will increase media literacy and make you a more effective news consumer."

Thomas White

In the following viewpoint, Thomas White maintains that media literacy is a powerful way for consumers to combat bias in the media. Media literacy is empowering, White argues, because it allows the consumer to analyze information from a variety of media. The number of media sources is growing, the author asserts, but this only benefits consumers if they have the tools to digest the information they receive from the news. The author offers several tips for improving one's media literacy, from varying sources of media to seeking slower—but more accurate—news reporting. White is a Global Academic Fellow at NYU Shanghai, focusing on writing. He graduated from New York University with a bachelor's and master's degree in politics and international affairs.

AS YOU READ, CONSIDER THE FOLLOWING QUESTIONS:
1. What is the definition of *media literacy*, according to the author?
2. As stated by White, what happens when people only get their news from one source?
3. Which networks reported inaccurate information about the 2012 US Supreme Court ruling on the Affordable Care Act, according to the author?

The media are biased. Fox News, MSNBC, the *New York Times*, the *Wall Street Journal*—they're all biased. They're biased in different ways, in varying degrees, and for various reasons. They're also, at times, voyeuristic, unprofessional, vapid, and incorrect. And all of this begs the question: how can one consume news without walking away either wrong or disenchanted?

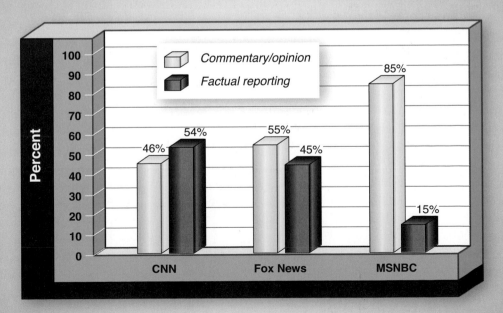

Types of Reporting on Major Cable News Networks, 2013

Taken from: Mark Jurkowitz, "Is MSNBC the Place for Opinion?," Pew Research Center, June 5, 2013. www.pewresearch.org.

A wise consumer gets news from a variety of sources. Social media outlets such as Twitter can easily disseminate misinformation.

In some ways, we are slaves to the news. But there are things that we can do as conscientious listeners, watchers, and readers of news that can make us more effective and knowledgeable about the world around us. It's called *media literacy* and it describes the set of skills we all have (or hope to have) that allow us to "access, analyze, evaluate, and communicate information" from a wide variety of media. It's the ability to discern fact from fluff, and information from entertainment. It's an important skill, like knowing how to read.

Why Is Media Literacy Important?

Being a conscientious news consumer is vital to the success of so many facets of everyday life. Understanding the issues helps keep those with power in check. Recognizing problems amidst a flurry of contradictory media messages is essential to letting governments know when we disagree and when we have a problem. Public opinion is only as powerful as our media literacy is sharp.

There are *so many* news outlets available to us today. Far more than ten, twenty, or fifty years ago. There are more TV news stations, websites, and an infinite number of blogs willing to impart their spin, their opinion, or their version of the facts. In a way, this can be beneficial to society, but only if we, as consumers, have the tools necessary to distinguish fact from the vast mountain of information at our fingertips.

Media is absolutely, undisputedly crucial to a successful democracy. It would be impossible to live in our world without it. But the media we have is far from perfect. And thus, there are things we can do to improve our media literacy and account for these deficiencies.

How to Improve Media Literacy

1. Vary our sources

Just as you wouldn't trust one professor to teach you your entire education (Mr. Feeny from [the TV show] *Boy Meets World* aside), getting your news from one source will skew your opinions and beliefs about important issues. Different outlets have different sets of advertisers, stockholders, and core viewers to please, creating biased news or dumbed down infotainment. Jon Stewart, for his part, has made a career poking fun at this absurdity.

Taking an individual source of news as one valuable piece of information out of many will give consumers more knowledge and a better understanding of the facts. So read the newspaper, listen to news radio, watch your local news, and test out different outlets, like the new Al Jazeera America, which just launched, promising to be controversial, hard-hitting, and focused on the facts. Find five to seven diverse sources that you enjoy and take in a few stories from each one, every single day.

2. Embrace bias

Bias can give us a better understanding of the news if we approach it in the right way. Different sources adopt different tones, highlight different facts, and discuss stories in different contexts. Watching the talking heads on Fox News and MSNBC characterize a presidential debate, you'd think they weren't watching the same thing. Reading, watching, and listening with a critical eye and an engaged mind will increase media literacy and make you a more effective news consumer.

FAST FACT

According to the Poynter Institute, a 2012 survey found that on a given day, 33 percent of Americans under the age of thirty get news from social networks, 34 percent watch TV news, and just 13 percent get news from print or digital newspapers.

It may also make you totally disenchanted by hundreds of news outlets, which operate seemingly under two completely different sets of facts. But the only way to understand the nuggets of truth inside them all is to watch and decide for yourself.

3. Slow news is far more accurate and reliable

The 24-hour news cycle has thrown out the window the idea that accurate news reporting is righteous. Instead, reporting news first (sometimes by mere seconds) is prized, especially on 24-hour cable news. Getting information quickly is one of the greatest gifts of our modern age, but when it comes to news, it shouldn't be at the expense of quality. It makes the whole industry look laughably inadequate when they misreport important news with such regularity and without apology—like when both CNN and Fox somehow got wrong the Supreme Court's Affordable Care Act ruling [in June 2012].

But why would the news outlets stop if it can help increase their ratings? They won't. So we have to be conscious of this and not let our desire to tweet the news before our friends override our desire to understand the facts.

4. Social media isn't #news

Social media can help incite a revolution. But that doesn't make it a legitimate source for news. Facebook and Twitter factoids, updates, and hashtags are no replacement for journalistic reporting, no matter how attractive a shortcut it may seem. And anyone who tries to tell you otherwise doesn't know what news is.

Like anything important, consuming news takes time and energy, and it should. It can't just be something we expect to absorb or understand through some crazy osmosis, whereby we increase our knowledge by being near others who've read or watched or listened to the news. It takes active presence, not passive acceptance. It requires you to question vigorously and reevaluate constantly.

Following these guidelines and becoming more media literate will help keep our politicians more honest, those with power more accountable, and our world more hopeful. Plus, it will make you look *really* smart at dinner parties.

> ## EVALUATING THE AUTHOR'S ARGUMENTS:
>
> In this viewpoint, Thomas White asserts that a media-literate public will hold those in power more accountable. On the basis of what you have read, what impact do you think media literacy could have on US politics?

Creating a Sixth Estate: A Critique of All Media

Stephen J.A. Ward

> "The sixth estate would . . . monitor and critique the ethical lapses of both mainstream and non-mainstream media."

In the following viewpoint, Stephen J.A. Ward contends that the public must criticize all media, not just the mainstream media. The public often accuses the mainstream media of bias while ignoring that of online media, Ward argues. Bloggers, websites, and media startups are often seen as grassroots and trendy, he contends, but they often escape public scrutiny and are allowed to operate with a lack of ethics. Online publishers have a responsibility to the public, Ward asserts, and should be held to the same standards expected of the mainstream media. Ward is director of the University of Oregon's journalism think tank the George S. Turnbull Center and an author of *The Invention of Journalism Ethics*, *Ethics and the Media*, and *Global Journalism Ethics*.

AS YOU READ, CONSIDER THE FOLLOWING QUESTIONS:

1. According to the author, how do online journalists compare their work to that of the mainstream media?

2. As stated by Ward, what happened to the family of Sunil Tripathi after Reddit.org shared a rumor about him online?
3. Ward proposes the creation of a sixth estate, which would comprise whom?

For over a decade, bloggers, web sites and trendy media start-ups have skewered the mainstream media for ethical lapses.

They have feasted on the mainstream's coverage biases and blind spots. Online media enthusiasts thump their chests: their work is democratic and from the grassroots, while mainstream media is elitist and arrogant.

Mainstream media "hide" facts from readers by gatekeeping; online media is cool, transparent, and honest about biases. They share everything in real time unlike the slow and paternalistic mediation of big media.

FAST FACT

The World Economic Forum ranking of the most significant global trends in 2014 placed the rapid spread of misinformation online as number ten.

It is time we blew up, logically, this self-serving, pompous attitude.

We need to expose the limitations, hypocrisy, and arrogance of any media worker, anywhere, including website operators who exhibit a scandalous lack of media ethics.

Digital Responsibilities

The ethics of publication is tough. It doesn't play favourites. It does not give anyone a "get out of ethics" card. Since publication can have harmful consequences, from cyber bullying to ruining reputations, any publisher can be called to account.

Online publishers have digital responsibilities—the responsibilities of citizens and professionals working with digital media.

Yet, some people seem to think that working online allows them to skirt editorial safeguards expected of the mainstream. Consider the actions of a group of online practitioners during the Boston Marathon bombing on April 15, 2013.

Online sites like Reddit, where people "vote up" stories, combined with tweeters and bloggers to form an online posse that set out to find a second suspect in the bombing. They took it upon themselves to act, in one swoop, as police, breaking news reporters, and vigilantes.

Not long ago, Jay Caspian Kang in the *New York Times Magazine* published a detailed account of this affair.

Here is what happened:

Near the time of the bombing, the family of a Sunil Tripathi, a Brown University student, had been missing for some time. The family was worried and looking for him. They set up a Facebook site asking people to help them find Sunil. They put a photo of him on the site. Later, his body was found in a river.

During the bombing, some people at Reddit.org, the self-described "front page of the Internet", and elsewhere on the Internet saw a resemblance between grainy police photos and the picture of Sunil Tripathi on the family's Facebook site. In the fast-paced world of the Internet, what started as speculation that Sunil might be a suspect quickly became a "fact." He was misidentified as the suspect.

The family suffered cruel online abuse. The family had to take down the Facebook site.

The so-called "wisdom of the crowd," and the vaunted democratic exercise of "crowdsourcing," became the undemocratic tyranny of the mob, unrestrained by "old-fashioned" mainstream values such as fairness and minimizing harm.

What is shocking was not just the mistake, but the superficial excuses given for the misidentification, after the fact. Also shocking was the lack of a sign that corrective policies would be introduced to prevent future mistakes.

In Kang's article, some of the writers who participated in this tragic affair tried to shrug off their digital responsibilities by taking a passive attitude: this is how the media world now works. Others argued that, by tweeting a rumor about Tripathi, they were not endorsing it. But sharing the rumor promoted the online belief that Sunil was the suspect.

Still others complained that it was the fault of the media platform—voting-up sites like Redditt are "content gnostic" or a "space for speculation." If content is not illegal, it isn't removed.

Public Opinion on the Reliability of News Organizations

Which statement better describes news organizations?

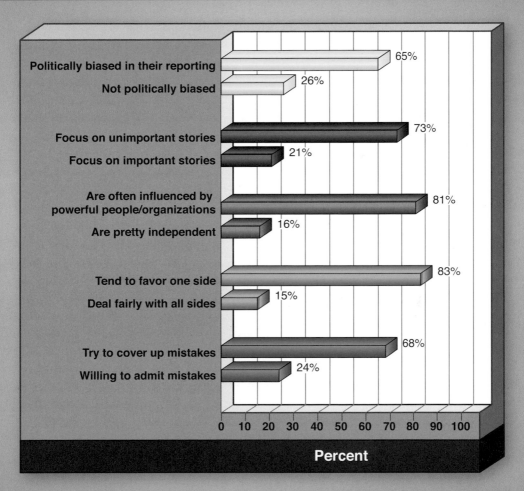

Note: Analysis based on telephone interviews conducted July 17–21, 2013, among a national sample of 1,480 adults, eighteen years of age or older, living in all fifty US states and the District of Columbia.

Taken from: Pew Research Center for the People and the Press, "Amid Criticism, Support for Media's 'Watchdog' Role Stands Out," August 8, 2013. www.people-press.org

A woman reads Reddit on a tablet computer. All media outlets should be held to the same standards of editorial and journalistic integrity as mainstream news outlets, according to media observers.

Moreover, the crowd that votes on stories dilutes personal responsibility to the point where no one in particular is responsible.

The "blame the platform" reasoning, based on escaping responsibility by becoming a face in the crowd, has justified many evils. There is something people online can do. We can refuse to join vigilante movements and rumor mongering. We can refuse to participate in Twitter storms where uncertainty exists and great harm is possible. Publishers of websites can introduce special policies that seriously restraint vigilante conduct online.

The morale is clear: Transparency and sharing of information online is an insufficient ethics for online publication. Such values should be tempered by a concern for accuracy, verification, and minimizing harm.

The problem, I fear, is that some online entrepreneurs are more interested in attracting crowds, creating a buzz, and making money than worrying about ethics. The best "cover" for such ambitions is to talk about the wondrous transparency and grassroots nature of their media, and contrast it with a caricature of mainstream media.

However, in Kang's article, it appeared that the Boston misidentification might lead to a more robust moral conscience. Erik Martin, Reddit general manager, apologized to the Tripathi family. He is quoted as saying: "After this week, which showed the best and the worst of Reddit's potential, we hope that Boston will also be where Reddit learns to be sensitive of its own power."

Indeed. We now need to talk about the power of leading online sites, not just the power of CNN or the *New York Times*.

Yet, five months later, the same online misidentification of suspects occurred during a mass shooting at a navy yard in Washington, D.C.

What will it take to get these people to take seriously their digital responsibilities?

A Sixth Estate

I call for the construction of a sixth estate. The fourth estate, which became our mainstream media, watchdog government. The fifth estate, alternative media, watchdog the fourth estate. The sixth estate would be composed of responsible media practitioners and concerned citizens. Their task: to monitor and critique the ethical lapses of both mainstream and non-mainstream media.

It is time to turn our attention to the ethical lapses—and resistance to ethics, per se—of any and all journalists. Let's turn up the heat on glib "new media" masters in the name of old-fashioned decency, while continuing to hold mainstream media to account.

It is time to create sixth estate networks that take media criticism to a new level. We need a daily aggregate of both good and bad ethical practice online, and we need to publicly name and shame those who refuse to be accountable for the harm they cause others.

Also, the sixth estate can support efforts to create a new media ethics that will outline our digital responsibilities as citizens, citizen journalists, and mainstream journalists.

We need to articulate the guiding principles and best practices.

The mantra of a sixth estate is: Seek accountability from all.

EVALUATING THE AUTHOR'S ARGUMENTS:

In this viewpoint, Stephen J.A. Ward asserts that the creation of a sixth estate would allow the public to hold mainstream media and alternative media accountable for their actions. Do you believe that the creation of a sixth estate would be effective in reducing media bias? Why or why not?

Balance and Bias

Ross Douthat

"We'd be better off . . . if our battered-but-still-powerful media establishment did more to . . . pursue a wider variety of journalistic ideals."

In the following viewpoint, Ross Douthat argues that the commitment to nonpartisanship and neutrality has harmed the journalism industry. In its attempts to reach an illusionary ideal of objectivity, the media have limited their ability to offer balanced news coverage, the author maintains. Douthat highlights the trend of Washington, DC–area journalists to consider the best legislation to be bipartisan and thus fair and objective. This does a disservice to the public, he asserts, because the media are favoring centrism for its own sake rather than the actual content of individual laws. Instead of focusing on neutrality, the author contends, the media could offer more balanced news by multiplying their perspectives and diversifying their coverage. Douthat is a *New York Times* columnist who focuses on politics and culture.

AS YOU READ, CONSIDER THE FOLLOWING QUESTIONS:

1. According to the author, what are the two ideological ideals of journalism?
2. How does the author define *bipartisanthink*?
3. As stated by Douthat, how do the mainstream media tend to cover social issues?

The traditional American mass media—the crumbling, Internet-besieged edifice of newspapers and news shows, magazines and roundtables and journalism schools—evolved to believe with equal vigor in two not entirely compatible ideals.

One is an ideal of balance, nonpartisanship and near-perfect neutrality—distilled to its essence, perhaps, by the former *Washington Post* editor Leonard Downie Jr.'s longstanding refusal to cast a vote, "so that I never make up my mind which party, candidate or ideology should be in power."

The other is a much more ideological ideal, which treats journalism as a kind of vanguard profession—fighting for the powerless against the powerful and leading America toward enlightenment.

Both of these visions have inspired great journalists and impressive publications. But many of the establishment media's worst habits arise from the doomed attempt to pursue both of them at once.

The Media Have Embraced "Bipartisanthink"

Consider, for instance, the Washington press's tendency toward what critics have dubbed "bipartisanthink"—in which journalists fetishize centrism and deal making, and assume that the best of all possible legislation, regardless of its actual content, is the kind that has both parties' fingerprints on it. By conflating the march of progress with the march of legislation through Congress, bipartisanthink allows journalists to take sides and root for particular outcomes without having to explicitly choose sides.

Usually this happens on fiscal issues, where the mainstream press's attitude for the last few years has often been: "We need a grand bargain and we don't care what is in it!" And usually bipartisanthink irritates liberals more than conservatives, because liberals sense—accurately enough—that many of the media personalities talking up, say, the Simpson-Bowles deficit plan would actually be perfectly happy with President Obama's deficit plan, but feel a professional obligation not to admit it. Conservatives, meanwhile, tend to be more frustrated by bipartisanthink's cousin, "leading the conversation." This is how the mainstream media tend to cover social issues, and it involves acting as a crusading vanguard while denying, often self-righteously, that anything of the sort is happening.

I'm borrowing the term from the *Daily Beast*'s Howard Kurtz, who used it to describe how the press (while also "being fair to all sides") should handle the aftermath of the Newtown shootings. The trouble is that when you set out to "lead" a conversation, you often end up deciding where it goes, which side wins the arguments and even who gets to participate. This was clear enough in Kurtz's own piece, which assumed that stricter gun control was the only rational policy response to Newtown. And it's been clear enough in all of the culturally charged debates—over guns and gay marriage, immigration and abortion—that have attracted media attention of late.

The Problem with "Leading the Conversation"

On these issues, an official journalistic commitment to neutrality coexists with the obvious ideological thrust of a thousand specific editorial choices: what kinds of questions are asked of which politicians; which stories get wall-to-wall coverage and which ones end up buried; which side is portrayed as aggressors and which side as the aggrieved party, and on and on and on.

"Leading the conversation" is how you end up with the major Sunday shows somehow neglecting to invite a single anti-amnesty politician on a weekend dominated by the immigration debate. It's how you end up with officially nonideological anchors and journalists lecturing social conservatives for being out of step with modern values. And it's how you end up with a press corps that went all-in for the supposed "war on women" having to be shamed and harassed—by two writers in particular, Kirsten Powers in *USA Today* and Mollie Ziegler Hemingway of GetReligion—into paying attention to the grisly case of a Philadelphia doctor whose methods of late-term abortion included snipping the spines of neonates after they were delivered.

> **FAST FACT**
>
> According to the Pew Research Center, newspaper membership in the Association of Opinion Journalists, representing editorial writers and columnists, decreased by 55 percent between 2006 and 2013.

Percent of respondents who agree that news organizations "keep leaders from doing things that shouldn't be done":

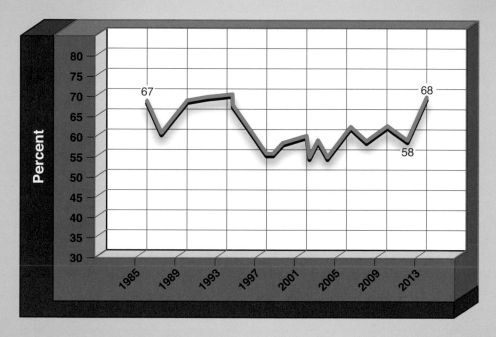

Note: Analysis based on telephone interviews conducted July 17–21, 2013, among a national sample of 1,480 adults, eighteen years of age or older, living in all fifty US states and the District of Columbia.

Taken from: Pew Research Center for the People and the Press, "Amid Criticism, Support for Media's 'Watchdog' Role Stands Out," August 8, 2013. www.people-press.org

As the last example suggests, the problem here isn't that American journalists are too quick to go on crusades. Rather, it's that the press's ideological blinders limit the kinds of crusades mainstream outlets are willing to entertain, and the formal commitment to neutrality encourages self-deception about what counts as crusading.

The core weakness of the mainstream media, in this sense, is less liberalism than parochialism. The same habits of mind that make bipartisanthink seem like the height of wisdom also make it easy to condescend to causes and groups that seem disreputable and to under-play stories that might vindicate them.

The best response to this problem probably doesn't involve dou-bling down on a quest for an illusory neutrality. We'd be better off, instead, if our battered-but-still-powerful media establishment did more to lean into the Internet era, which for all its challenges offers opportunities as well—the chance to multiply perspectives, to pro-mote a diverse (and, yes, sometimes competing) array of causes and to pursue a wider variety of journalistic ideals.

EVALUATING THE AUTHOR'S ARGUMENTS:

In this viewpoint, Ross Douthat contends that the media should strive to diversify their coverage. Do you agree that media balance and diversity would benefit the journal-ism industry more so than striving for neutrality? Why or why not?

The Public Can Fight Media Bias by Recognizing It

Rini Sampath

"Though we might trust the media with inform-ing us of the news, gather-ing the most correct ver-sion of the facts is still up to us."

In the following viewpoint, Rini Sampath argues that the public plays an important role in media bias. While the media has a responsibility to report the news, Sampath contends, the public must understand that journalists are human and thus bias will exist. It is unfair to hold journalists to an unattainable standard of fairness and bal-ance, the author maintains. News sources should admit to their positions, the author argues, and then it is up to the public to decipher the news that they are digesting and learn to recognize its biases. At the time this viewpoint was written, Sampath was an international relations student at the University of Southern California in Los Angeles.

AS YOU READ, CONSIDER THE FOLLOWING QUESTIONS:

1. According to the author, why do media outlets often sensationalize stories?
2. What liberal movement gained the favor of the media, as stated by Sampath?

3. In a poll cited by the author, which viewers were the most informed about current events?

Because of the attacks on the American embassy in Benghazi, [Libya, in September 2012] former Secretary of State Hillary Clinton found herself in front of the firing squad known as Congress in a special hearing [on January 23, 2013,] to determine if her actions directly led to the deaths of several Americans.

As a reputable news source, Fox News decided to cover the hearings, yet it was almost impossible to ignore the obvious bias the network has against liberal ideologies.

Holding the Media to Unattainable Standards

Pick up a newspaper, watch a segment of the news or tune into the radio station, and a realization will transpire: You're either reading, watching or hearing a human.

And ultimately, human beings err. Human beings make blanket statements and rude comments. They lie, cheat and tell half-truths. Somewhere in all of this human error lie journalists—individuals who are paid to remain unbiased and provide society with the facts.

The Rachel Maddow Show is a news and opinion program with an openly liberal political bias. Because no media is free of bias, the public should focus on the content and discern the facts for themselves.

Unfortunately, society cannot hold humans to unattainable standards of fairness and balance. Part of the problem is that the public argues that the media must be completely unbiased, while simultaneously thirsting for riveting news stories and explosive headlines.

Viewership depends on the nature of stories, and more often than not, media outlets sensationalize stories to increase viewership. For instance, the saying "if it bleeds, it leads" emerged from the increase in crime reporting among news organizations.

Examining Media Bias

But is it entirely wrong for news outlets to pay the bills using these tactics—especially when society seemingly would much rather feel entertained than intellectually stimulated?

Admittedly, the media's actions are unforgivable in some instances. Portraying First Lady Michelle Obama as "Obama's Baby Mama" on Fox News is inappropriate for all American audiences. And condensing Clinton's congressional testimony into four mocking bullet points such as, "Hey guys—this stuff is hard!" is both inaccurate and disrespectful.

FAST FACT

According to Public Policy Polling, Fox News ranked as the most trusted news source in 2014, with 35 percent of Americans trusting it more than any other TV news source; however, it was also the least trusted source, with 33 percent trusting it less than any other.

And though conservative media outlets are often critiqued for their ridiculous proclamations, liberal news sources must also be examined.

The Western Center for Journalism points out the copious ways in which media has tipped in favor of leftist movements such as Occupy Wall Street. Moreover, *Huffington Post* reporter Michael Calderone compares the strong liberal opinions of MSNBC hosts to conservative Fox News hosts.

Human beings obviously have opinions, but media outlets cannot pretend to be unbiased when their shows and hosts push a specific sort of agenda. As long as these news sources admit to their positions, then

NPR Listeners Are the Most Knowledgeable About the News

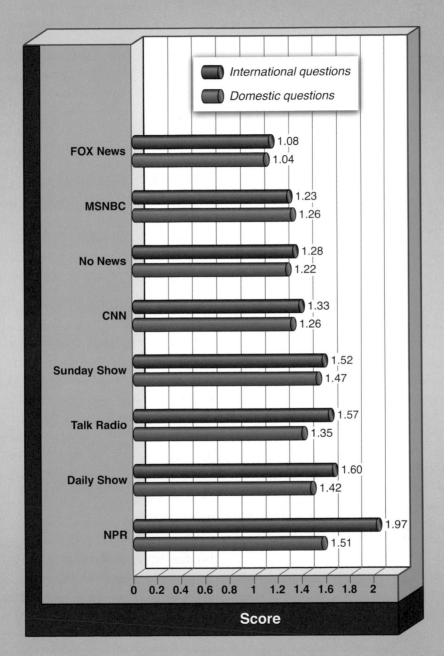

International questions
Domestic questions

Source	International	Domestic
FOX News	1.08	1.04
MSNBC	1.23	1.26
No News	1.28	1.22
CNN	1.33	1.26
Sunday Show	1.52	1.47
Talk Radio	1.57	1.35
Daily Show	1.60	1.42
NPR	1.97	1.51

Score: 0 0.2 0.4 0.6 0.8 1 1.2 1.4 1.6 1.8 2

Note: Scores above based on number of correct answers about international news and domestic affairs on a nationwide survey of 1,185 adults conducted February 2012.

Taken from: Fairleigh Dickinson University's PublicMind, "What You Know Depends on What You Watch: Current Events Knowledge Across Popular News Sources," May 3, 2012.

the public will better understand the nature of the news that they're digesting rather than fall sway to a skewed version of events.

The Public Must Identify Media Bias

A study conducted by Fairleigh Dickinson University polled a variety of viewers using current events questions. They determined that NPR [National Public Radio] viewers were among the best informed, and viewers who preferred watching Fox News were the worst informed.

Perhaps this information shows that the public may not even have to focus on bias in media, but rather on the content and depth of the information shared. The American people should feel capable of answering questions regarding economic sanctions or the level of unemployment as citizens of this nation. But if news sources fail to provide the people with the objective facts necessary to participate in energizing conversation, they fail society altogether. If the only things the American people can discuss after watching a segment of Fox News are gossipy, mean-spirited details about the Obama family, a drastic change is necessary.

One cannot watch Fox News or MSNBC and expect completely impartial reporting. No matter how hard a journalist might try, their individual beliefs will almost always manage to creep its way into a story, especially if an organization promotes a particular angle.

Though we might trust the media with informing us of the news, gathering the most correct version of the facts is still up to us.

EVALUATING THE AUTHOR'S ARGUMENTS:

In this viewpoint, Rini Sampath asserts that the public holds the media to an unattainable level of unbiased reporting. Do you agree with Sampath's argument that the public should expect some level of bias in the news media? Explain your answer.

The Best Way to Fight Media Bias Is to Avoid the News

Rolf Dobelli

"Most of us do not yet understand that news is to the mind what sugar is to the body . . . toxic."

In the following viewpoint, Rolf Dobelli argues that the public should limit its media consumption. The news business is inherently misleading, the author contends, and human beings are not rational enough for regular exposure to the press. People often get anxious when they are cut off from the daily flow of the news, he asserts, and it is very difficult for them to discern relevant information. Journalism is important to society, the author believes, but important findings do not have to arrive in the form of news. Instead, he maintains, the public should look to in-depth journal articles and books in order to find new information. Dobelli cofounded getAbstract, the world's largest publisher of compressed business knowledge, and is the author of *The Art of Thinking Clearly.*

AS YOU READ, CONSIDER THE FOLLOWING QUESTIONS:

1. Why does Dobelli compare absorbing the news to eating candy?
2. According to the author, what are the most important news stories?

In the past few decades, the fortunate among us have recognised the hazards of living with an overabundance of food (obesity, diabetes) and have started to change our diets. But most of us do not yet understand that news is to the mind what sugar is to the body. News is easy to digest. The media feeds us small bites of trivial matter, tidbits that don't really concern our lives and don't require thinking. That's why we experience almost no saturation. Unlike reading books and long magazine articles (which require thinking), we can swallow limitless quantities of news flashes, which are bright-coloured candies for the mind. Today, we have reached the same point in relation to information that we faced 20 years ago in regard to food. We are beginning to recognise how toxic news can be.

News Misleads

Take the following event (borrowed from [essayist] Nassim Taleb). A car drives over a bridge, and the bridge collapses. What does the news media focus on? The car. The person in the car. Where he came from. Where he planned to go. How he experienced the crash (if he survived). But that is all irrelevant. What's relevant? The structural stability of the bridge. That's the underlying risk that has been lurking, and could lurk in other bridges. But the car is flashy, it's dramatic, it's a person (non-abstract), and it's news that's cheap to produce. News leads us to walk around with the completely wrong risk map in our heads. So terrorism is over-rated. Chronic stress is under-rated. The collapse of Lehman Brothers is overrated. Fiscal irresponsibility is under-rated. Astronauts are over-rated. Nurses are under-rated.

We are not rational enough to be exposed to the press. Watching an airplane crash on television is going to change your attitude toward that risk, regardless of its real probability. If you think you can compensate with the strength of your own inner contemplation, you are wrong. Bankers and economists—who have powerful incentives to compensate for news-borne hazards—have shown that they cannot. The only solution: cut yourself off from news consumption entirely.

News Is Irrelevant

Out of the approximately 10,000 news stories you have read in the last 12 months, name one that—because you consumed it—allowed you to make a better decision about a serious matter affecting your life, your career or your business. The point is: the consumption of news is irrelevant to you. But people find it very difficult to recognise what's relevant. It's much easier to recognise what's new. The relevant versus the new is the fundamental battle of the current age. Media organisations want you to believe that news offers you some sort of a competitive advantage. Many fall for that. We get anxious when we're cut off from the flow of news. In reality, news consumption is a competitive disadvantage. The less news you consume, the bigger the advantage you have.

News Has No Explanatory Power

News items are bubbles popping on the surface of a deeper world. Will accumulating facts help you understand the world? Sadly, no. The relationship is inverted. The important stories are non-stories:

"You know, it's O.K. to skip a news cycle."

slow, powerful movements that develop below journalists' radar but have a transforming effect. The more "news factoids" you digest, the less of the big picture you will understand. If more information leads to higher economic success, we'd expect journalists to be at the top of the pyramid. That's not the case.

News Is Toxic to Your Body

[News] constantly triggers the limbic system. Panicky stories spur the release of cascades of glucocorticoid (cortisol). This deregulates your immune system and inhibits the release of growth hormones. In other words, your body finds itself in a state of chronic stress. High glucocorticoid levels cause impaired digestion, lack of growth (cell, hair, bone), nervousness and susceptibility to infections. The other potential side-effects include fear, aggression, tunnel-vision and desensitisation.

News Increases Cognitive Errors

News feeds the mother of all cognitive errors: confirmation bias. In the words of [tycoon] Warren Buffett: "What the human being is best at doing is interpreting all new information so that their prior conclusions remain intact." News exacerbates this flaw. We become prone to overconfidence, take stupid risks and misjudge opportunities. It also exacerbates another cognitive error: the story bias. Our brains crave stories that "make sense"—even if they don't correspond to reality. Any journalist who writes, "The market moved because of X" or "the company went bankrupt because of Y" is an idiot. I am fed up with this cheap way of "explaining" the world.

News Inhibits Thinking

Thinking requires concentration. Concentration requires uninterrupted time. News pieces are specifically engineered to interrupt you. They are like viruses that steal attention for their own purposes. News makes us shallow thinkers. But it's worse than that. News severely affects memory. There are two types of memory. Long-range memory's capacity is nearly infinite, but working memory is limited to a

People who consume vast amounts of news each day run the risk of becoming unable to distinguish relevant news from irrelevant news.

certain amount of slippery data. The path from short-term to long-term memory is a choke-point in the brain, but anything you want to understand must pass through it. If this passageway is disrupted, nothing gets through. Because news disrupts concentration, it weakens comprehension. Online news has an even worse impact. In a 2001 study two scholars in Canada showed that comprehension declines as the number of hyperlinks in a document increases. Why? Because whenever a link appears, your brain has to at least make the choice not to click, which in itself is distracting. News is an intentional interruption system.

News Works Like a Drug

As stories develop, we want to know how they continue. With hundreds of arbitrary storylines in our heads, this craving is increasingly compelling and hard to ignore. Scientists used to think that the dense connections formed among the 100 billion neurons inside our skulls were largely fixed by the time we reached adulthood. Today we know that this is not the case. Nerve cells routinely break old connections and form new ones. The more news we consume, the more we exercise the neural circuits devoted to skimming and multitasking while ignoring those used for reading deeply and thinking with profound focus. Most news consumers—even if they used to be avid book readers—have lost the ability to absorb lengthy articles or books. After four, five pages they get tired, their concentration vanishes, they become restless. It's not because they got older or their schedules became more onerous. It's because the physical structure of their brains has changed.

News Wastes Time

If you read the newspaper for 15 minutes each morning, then check the news for 15 minutes during lunch and 15 minutes before you go to bed, then add five minutes here and there when you're at work, then count distraction and refocusing time, you will lose at least half a day every week. Information is no longer a scarce commodity. But attention is. You are not that irresponsible with your money, reputation or health. Why give away your mind?

News Makes People Passive

News stories are overwhelmingly about things you cannot influence. The daily repetition of news about things we can't act upon makes us passive. It grinds us down until we adopt a worldview that is pessimistic, desensitised, sarcastic and fatalistic. The scientific term is "learned helplessness". It's a bit of a stretch, but I would not be surprised if news consumption at least partially contributes to the widespread disease of depression.

News Kills Creativity

Finally, things we already know limit our creativity. This is one reason that mathematicians, novelists, composers and entrepreneurs often produce their most creative works at a young age. Their brains enjoy a wide, uninhabited space that emboldens them to come up with and pursue novel ideas. I don't know a single truly creative mind who is a news junkie—not a writer, not a composer, mathematician, physician, scientist, musician, designer, architect or painter. On the other hand, I know a bunch of viciously uncreative minds who consume news like drugs. If you want to come up with old solutions, read news. If you are looking for new solutions, don't.

Society needs journalism—but in a different way. Investigative journalism is always relevant. We need reporting that polices our institutions and uncovers truth. But important findings don't have to arrive in the form of news. Long journal articles and in-depth books are good, too.

I have now gone without news for four years, so I can see, feel and report the effects of this freedom first-hand: less disruption, less anxiety, deeper thinking, more time, more insights. It's not easy, but it's worth it.

EVALUATING THE AUTHOR'S ARGUMENTS:

In this viewpoint, Rolf Dobelli claims that the public should limit its consumption of the news because of its harmful mental and physical effects. Why might someone argue that regular consumption of the news is beneficial?

More Support of Public Media Will Reduce Media Bias

"Public media outlets do a better job of providing news and information for a democracy."

Seth Ashley

In the following viewpoint, Seth Ashley argues that a structural bias is inherent in the US commercial media system because the market favors speech that is agreeable to its financial interests. The public has become accustomed to hearing voices that support this status quo, the author contends, without realizing that they are being misinformed. Research shows that public media outlets do a better job of providing news, Ashley maintains, and public media consumers have higher levels of knowledge about current events than consumers of mainstream media. In order to improve society, Ashley believes that the United States must invest in public media. Ashley is an assistant professor of communication at Boise State University in Idaho.

AS YOU READ, CONSIDER THE FOLLOWING QUESTIONS:
1. According to the author, how much did the Corporation for Public Broadcasting lose from its budget in 2013?
2. How much do public media receive per American each year, as stated by Ashley?
3. Compared to the United States, what is the range of per capita spending on public media in other countries, according to Ashley?

We haven't heard much about public media since Big Bird's spotlight in last year's [2012] presidential debates, but it remains one of our most trusted public institutions and our second favorite use of tax dollars after military defense. Now, the Corporation for Public Broadcasting is set to lose five percent of its already meager budget thanks to the sequester [2013 US federal government budget cuts]. This comes at a time when we should actually be spending more on what has proven to be one of the best investments we can make as a society.

Investing in Public Media

Unfortunately, even proponents of public media often do a poor job of making the case for public media, which currently receives about $1.39 per American per year, most of which gets distributed to local stations to help cover their costs. Rather than putting public media on the chopping block yet again, it's time to shift the debate to reflect reality.

First, when we compare the U.S. to any other developed nation, we see that we have always been alone in allowing the bulk of our news and information, the lifeblood of democracy, to come from commercial outlets funded primarily by advertising. With the rise of broadcasting in

> **FAST FACT**
>
> According to the 2011 report "Public Media and Political Independence," Norway spends $133.57 per person on public media, almost one hundred times the figure for the United States.

How much do you trust each organization? (percent responding "a great deal"):

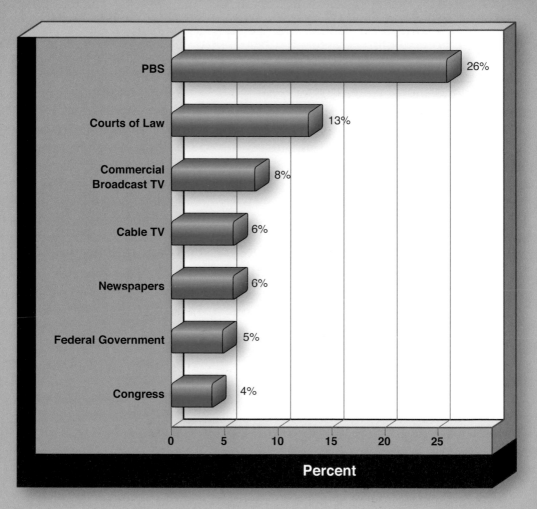

Note: Data from Harris Interactive Trust QuickQuery, February 2012.

Taken from: Public Broadcasting System, "Today's PBS," 2012. www.pbs.org.

the 1920s, the emerging industry worked to guarantee licensing policies that would be favorable to commercial interests and went out of its way to quash the calls for the kind of nonprofit, noncommercial broadcasting that was the norm in Britain and other

European nations. Path dependence makes it difficult to depart from the status quo.

Neoliberalism has not been kind to public media generally, but many outlets still manage to thrive around the world, notably the BBC, which despite the assault by the Rupert Murdoch camp, remains a vital institution in British life. Today, the majority of developed nations contribute significant state resources to public media, and various mechanisms help preserve their independence from political influence, such as multi-year funding plans. A 2011 report, "Public Media and Political Independence," found that per capita spending on public media in other countries ranges from $30 to more than $130 per year.

Quality Journalism Benefits the Public

Second, critics of federal funding for public media suggest that there already is an abundance of media to choose from, making public media unnecessary. What these critics mean is that there is an abundance of commercial media outlets controlled by a handful of profit-oriented corporations. "Market failure" is the term used to describe the dearth of quality, independent journalism among companies that prefer to serve up cheap reality television and talk shows in order to make money. Quality journalism is a public good that benefits everyone—similar to clean air and national defense—and requires extensive public funding. The founders of the republic knew this and granted enormous printing and postal subsidies that helped sustain journalism through the 19th century. One study calculates these early subsidies to be equivalent to $30 billion today.

Today, the independent blogosphere contributes to democratic discourse but does not have the resources to do the kind of original reporting we need.

Third, plenty of evidence suggests that public media outlets do a better job of providing news and information for a democracy. For example, a well-known 2003 University of Maryland study found that consumers of NPR and PBS had fewer misperceptions related to the war in Iraq than consumers of commercial media. More recently, a May 2012 survey from Fairleigh Dickinson University found that NPR listeners have higher levels of knowledge of international current

In the United States the majority of news is delivered by commercial news outlets. Yet studies have shown that public media outlets—such as National Public Radio and the Public Broadcasting System—do a better job of providing balanced news and information.

events than consumers of mainstream commercial outlets. And countries with strong public media systems have better records of civic knowledge and engagement than the U.S. regardless of differences in education level and other demographic data.

Commercial Media Have a Structural Bias

Fourth, American public media are often subject to charges of political bias and imbalance, but these are often matters of perspective. This type of bias is in the eye of the beholder. What is less subjective is the structural bias built into a predominantly commercial media system. The market favors speech that is favorable to the market, and we become so used to hearing voices that support this status quo that anything else seems radical. It's easy to see that a media system of government propaganda controlled by officials is anathema to democratic values, but how is a predominantly commercial system controlled by profit motives any better?

We must remember that there is nothing natural or inevitable about our media system, which is structured through laws and policies that favor commercial interests. The U.S. system of broadcast licensing, for example, in which broadcasters are granted free use of the supposedly publicly owned airwaves, has been called a $70 billion giveaway. FCC commissioner Michael Copps told the *New York Times* that he hopes the Internet "doesn't travel down the same road of special interest consolidation and gate-keeper control that other media and telecommunications industries—radio, television, film and cable— have traveled. What an historic tragedy it would be," he said, "to let that fate befall the dynamism of the Internet."

Communication policy historically has been viewed as a technical matter to be handled by experts and administrators, not by democratic choice. It's time for that to change. The benefits of public media are widely acknowledged by Americans of all political stripes, and in our media-saturated information age, our ability to facilitate democratic media structures and institutions will play a role in deciding the fate of democracy itself.

> **EVALUATING THE AUTHOR'S ARGUMENTS:**
>
> In this viewpoint, Seth Ashley claims that supporting public media would reduce biased news coverage in the United States. Why might someone argue that investing in public media would not have an impact on media bias?

Facts About Media Bias

Editor's note: These facts can be used in reports to add credibility when making important points or claims.

Perceptions of Media Bias and the Role of the Press

According to the Pew Research Center:

- In 2012, the percentage of Americans who believed that news coverage showed a great deal of political bias reached 37 percent, while 30 percent thought there was just a fair amount. Only 21 percent said there was not too much bias, and 10 percent believed there was none at all.
- In 1989 about a quarter of both Republicans and Democrats said there was a "great deal of political bias in the news." In 2012 they were no longer in agreement as nearly half (49 percent) of Republicans cited a great deal of bias versus about a third (32 percent) of Democrats.
- Americans are far more critical of the press today than they were in 1985, when just 34 percent of survey respondents believed that news organizations often published inaccurate stories. By 2011 that figure had nearly doubled to 66 percent of Americans.
- Americans are less critical of their preferred news sources; only 30 percent of respondents said that the news sources they use the most often put out inaccurate stories.
- Fifty-three percent of Americans in 1985 said the press was often influenced by powerful people and organizations. That figure reached 80 percent in 2011.
- Fifty-three percent of Americans in 1985 felt that news organizations tended to favor one side over another on political and social issues. That figure had risen to 77 percent by 2011.
- Despite the rising criticism, Americans still trust the information they get from local and national news organizations more than what they hear from the government or corporations, with 69

percent saying they trust local news organizations and 59 percent trusting national news organizations.

- In contrast, people trust information from federal government agencies 44 percent of the time, from corporations 41 percent of the time, and from political candidates 29 percent of the time.

According to the Gallup polling organization:

- Republicans are far less trusting of the news media than are Democrats. In 2013, only 33 percent of Republicans expressed "a great deal" or "a fair amount" of trust in the media, while 60 percent of Democrats did.
- Independents are more trusting of the media than Republicans, but not by much. In 2013, among Independents, 37 percent said they trust news organizations "a great deal" or "a fair amount."

According to the Indiana University School of Journalism:

- In a 2013 survey of journalists, 60 percent thought that the field of journalism was going in the wrong direction; 23 percent thought it was going in the right direction, and 17 percent did not know.
- Concerning the role of news media in the United States, 69 percent of journalists believe that it is extremely important that the news media analyze complex problems in society, and 78 percent say that investigating government claims is an extremely important journalistic function.

According to the Oxford Internet Institute:

- In a 2013 study, British Internet users showed less trust in TV news and newspapers than nonusers or ex-users of the Internet.
- The same study found that only 14 percent of next-generation Internet users considered television essential for getting information while 30 percent of non- and ex-users valued television as a news source. Among first-generation Internet users, 18 percent considered television important.

Liberal and Conservative Media Bias

According to the Indiana University School of Journalism:

- In 2013, just 7 percent of journalists reported being Republicans, as opposed to 26 percent who identified as Republicans in 1971.
- Self-identifying Democrats accounted for 28 percent of journalists in 2013. The majority of journalists—50 percent—called themselves Independents in 2013.

According to the University of Texas:

- Republicans are more likely than Democrats to get news from an opposing point of view. Just 26 percent of Democrats will routinely seek news from a source that leans to the right, while 43 percent of Republicans will routinely turn to a left-leaning source.

According to the Pew Research Center:

- Fifty-eight percent of conservative Republicans and 73 percent of moderate or other Republicans in 2012 preferred to get political news with a neutral point of view rather than with their own point of view.
- In the same year, 62 percent of liberal Democrats preferred political news with no expressed point of view, as did 58 percent of moderate or more conservative Democrats.
- In analysis of news coverage of the 2012 presidential campaign, 36 percent of CNN's coverage of Mitt Romney depicted him negatively, while just 21 percent of the same network's coverage of Barack Obama was negative.
- Fox News showed a much greater preference for Romney, with just 12 percent of its coverage of him being negative, while 46 percent of its stories on Obama had a negative tone.
- MSNBC, however, exhibited an even greater bias by depicting Romney negatively in 71 percent of its stories while Obama was portrayed negatively in only 15 percent.

According to Public Policy Polling:

- Sixty-nine percent of Republicans in 2014 named Fox News their most trusted news source. Among Democrats there was more disagreement; the greatest number—21 percent—said PBS was their most trusted source, while CNN and ABC News each were favored by 18 percent, and CBS and MSNBC by 12 percent.

- The same study reported that 57 percent of Democrats said Fox News was their least trusted news source, while the highest percentage of Republicans (38 percent) considered MSNBC their least trusted source.

Media Bias and Public Media

According to New York University's Department of Media, Culture, and Communication:

- In a multinational comparison of public and private media organizations in 2009, researchers found that public television gave more attention to public affairs and international news than did commercial media channels.
- The same study also found that public news media encouraged a higher level of news consumption than did their commercial counterparts.

According to the Pew Research Center:

- Of those people who regularly get their news from National Public Radio, 72 percent say they prefer a news source that does not have a political point of view. That preference is shared by 63 percent of local news audiences, 56 percent of people who rely on CNN for their news, and 53 percent of those who tune in to Fox News.

According to Public Policy Polling:

- In a 2014 study of eight TV news outlets, PBS was the only one that a majority of Americans trusted, with 57 percent saying they trusted it and 24 percent saying they did not. Fox News came in second and CBS News third, with 44 percent and 39 percent, respectively.

Organizations to Contact

The editors have compiled the following list of organizations concerned with the issues debated in this book. The descriptions are derived from materials provided by the organizations. All have publications or information available for interested readers. The list was compiled on the date of publication of the present volume; the information provided here may change. Be aware that many organizations take several weeks or longer to respond to inquiries, so allow as much time as possible for the receipt of requested materials.

Accuracy in Media (AIM)
4350 East West Hwy., Suite 555
Bethesda, MD 20814
(202) 264-4401 • fax: (202) 364-4098
e-mail: info@aim.org
website: www.aim.org

Accuracy in Media is a nonprofit organization whose mission is to promote accuracy, fairness, and balance in the media. This media watchdog critiques biased news stories and reports on important issues that have received slanted coverage. AIM works to expose media bias that is politically motivated, teach the public to think critically about news sources, and hold the mainstream press accountable for misreporting. Its website features reports, blogs, and multimedia resources.

Center for Media and Public Affairs (CMPA)
933 N. Kenmore Street, Suite 405
Arlington, VA 22201
(571) 319-0029 • fax: (571) 319-0034
e-mail: mail@cmpa.com
website: www.cmpa.com

Founded in 1985, the Center for Media and Public Affairs is a nonprofit research and educational organization that conducts scientific studies of the media. The goal of the nonpartisan organization is to provide empirical research for ongoing debates over media coverage. CMPA aims to bridge the gap between academic research and the broader spheres of media and public policy. The organization's website offers access to its studies and books as well as its yearly media monitor.

Center for Media Literacy (CML)
22837 Pacific Coast Hwy., #472
Malibu, CA 90265
(310) 804-3985
website: www.medialit.com

The Center for Media Literacy is an educational organization that supports and promotes media literacy. It works to help citizens develop critical thinking skills in a global media culture. The ultimate goal of CML is to teach citizens to understand and analyze content in all media forms. Its website includes a media literacy kit, newsletter, online reference center, and links to its interviews and events.

Fairness and Accuracy in Reporting (FAIR)
124 W. 30th Street, Suite 201
New York, NY 10001
(212) 633-6700 • fax: (212) 727-7668
e-mail: fair@fair.org
website: www.fair.org

Founded in 1986, FAIR is a national media-watch group that offers documented criticism of media bias and censorship. The organization advocates for greater diversity in the press and scrutinizes media practices that disregard public interest. FAIR works to expose neglected news stories and defend journalists from censorship. The organization works with both activists and journalists and encourages the public to become media activists. FAIR publishes a magazine of media criticism titled *Extra!* and also produces the weekly radio program *CounterSpin*.

Media Matters for America
PO Box 52155
Washington, DC 20091
(202) 756-4100
website: http://mediamatters.org

Founded in 2004, Media Matters for America is a nonprofit progressive research and information center dedicated to monitoring conservative bias in the US media. It analyzes print, broadcast, cable, radio, and Internet media outlets for conservatively biased misinformation. News articles, research, and multimedia resources can be found on the Media Matters website.

Media Research Center (MRC)
1900 Campus Commons Dr., Suite 600
Reston, VA 20191
(517) 267-3500 • fax: (517) 375-0099
website: www.mrc.org

Founded in 1987, the Media Research Center is a media watchdog organization with a mission to expose liberally biased media coverage. The MRC uses cutting-edge news monitoring capabilities to educate Americans about liberal bias in the media. The organization comprises a News Analysis Division, Business and Media Institute, Culture and Media Institute, and CNSNews.com, an online news resource. The MRC's website features social media links, newsletters, research, and commentary.

Media Watch
PO Box 618
Santa Cruz, CA 95061
(831) 423-6355
e-mail: info@mediawatch.com
website: www.mediawatch.com

Media Watch is an nonprofit educational organization that aims to keep citizens involved in creating media that serve the needs of the public. The mission of the organization is to challenge abusive stereotypes and biased information found in the media through education and action. Media Watch endorses media literacy as part of the public education system and provides monthly newsletters to help create more-informed media consumers. The organization opposes any form of censorship. Media Watch produces video projects, newsletters, and blog postings on its website.

MediaChannel
PO Box 677
New York, NY 10035

website: www.mediachannel.org

MediaChannel is a nonprofit organization focused on the cultural, political, and social impacts of the media. The organization works to provide information from diverse perspectives that provokes debate, collaboration, action, and citizen engagement in holding the media accountable. MediaChannel seeks to develop an internationally oriented media and democracy movement through a network of affiliates. The organization's website offers global commentary and analysis as well as multimedia resources.

National Coalition Against Censorship (NCAC)

19 Fulton Street, Suite 407
New York, NY 10038
(212) 807-6222 • fax: (212) 807-6245
e-mail: ncac@ncac.org
website: www.ncac.org

The National Coalition Against Censorship was formed more than forty years ago in response to the 1973 Supreme Court decision in *Miller v. California*, which narrowed First Amendment protections for sexually oriented expression. The mission of NCAC is to promote freedom of thought. The organization opposes censorship in all forms and engages in advocacy and education to support First Amendment principles. NCAC has fostered an alliance of more than fifty literary, artistic, religious, educational, labor, and civil liberties groups across the nation.

Nieman Foundation

One Francis Ave.
Cambridge, MA 02138
(617) 495-2237
website: http://nieman.harvard.edu

Established in 1938, the Nieman Foundation at Harvard University is the oldest fellowship program for journalists in the world. The foundation publishes the quarterly magazine *Nieman Reports*, which is devoted to examining the practice of journalism. The foundation is also home to the Nieman Storyboard, an online exploration of narrative journalism. The foundation has established the Nieman Journalism Lab, which aims to help journalists make the transition to digital journalism while maintaining high journalistic standards. Its website offers the foundation's annual reports as well as links to its publications and programs.

Pew Research Center for the People and the Press
1615 L Street NW, Suite 700
Washington, DC 20036
(202) 419-4300 • fax: (202) 419-4349
website: www.people-press.org

The Pew Research Center for the People and the Press is a nonpartisan research organization that conducts public-opinion polling, demographic research, media-content analysis, and other empirical social science research. The center provides independent public-opinion survey research about Americans' attitudes toward politics and policy. Its reports examine long-term trends in political values, views on policy issues, and news interest. The center's website provides media news, as well as research about the state of the news media.

Poynter Institute
801 Third Street South
St. Petersburg, FL 33701
(727) 821-9494
website: www.poynter.org

The Poynter Institute is a school dedicated to teaching journalists and media leaders excellence and integrity in journalism. Poynter promotes journalism that informs citizens and enlightens public discourse. The institute develops training for newsroom professionals and educators. Poynter also offers programs for elementary, middle, high school, and college students. Its website features media news as well as links to in-person and online media training.

For Further Reading

Books

Alsultany, Evelyn. *Arabs and Muslims in the Media: Race and Representation After 9/11.* New York: New York University Press, 2012. In this book, the author examines how TV dramas, news organizations, and advertising in the United States have represented Arabs, Muslims, Arab Americans, and Muslim Americans since 9/11. She finds that more-diverse representations do not reduce racial stereotyping, and she believes seemingly positive images in the media can also lead to exclusion and inequality.

Cupp, S.E. *Losing Our Religion: Why the Liberal Media Want to Tell You What to Think, Where to Pray, and How to Live.* New York: Threshold, 2011. A media commentator takes a look at US media coverage of Christianity. The author believes there is a culture war in the United States and that the liberal media are fighting to marginalize Christianity and Judeo-Christian values.

D'Alessio, Dave. *Media Bias in Presidential Election Coverage, 1948–2008: Evaluation via Formal Measurement.* Lanham, MD: Lexington Books, 2012. A communications scientist analyzes presidential election coverage in the US media over a sixty-year period. In addition the author explores the nature of the journalism industry and how the public perceives news coverage.

Falk, Erika. *Women for President: Media Bias in Nine Campaigns.* 2nd ed. Urbana: University of Illinois Press, 2010. A communications expert analyzes gender bias in US media coverage of women presidential candidates. She looks at the campaigns of nine women—from 1872 through 2008—and finds that the media portray female candidates as incompetent for the job and often ignore or belittle their ideas.

Goldberg, Bernard. *Bias: A CBS Insider Exposes How the Media Distort the News.* Rev. ed. Washington, DC: Regnery, 2014. In this book, an Emmy Award–winning journalist exposes US media bias from an insider's point of view. The author writes that during the time that he worked as a reporter, the media far too often ignored their primary mission of objective reporting and consistently provided liberally biased coverage.

Huff, Mickey, and Andy Lee Roth, eds. *Censored 2015: Inspiring We the People; The Top Censored Stories and Media Analysis of 2013–2014*. New York: Seven Stories, 2014. This is Project Censored's annual yearbook of the top twenty-five most censored stories in the press as voted on by activists, scholars, and media workers. The goal of the annual project is to inform readers about stories that were underreported, or not reported at all, due to media bias and self-censorship.

Kuypers, Jim A. *Partisan Journalism: A History of Media Bias in the United States*. Lanham, MD: Rowman and Littlefield, 2013. A communications professor looks at bias in the US media throughout history. He finds that US journalism was founded in partisan roots, not objectivity. The mission of the industry has changed throughout history, he argues, but trends are showing that it is returning to its original partisan foundations.

Ladd, Jonathan M. *Why Americans Hate the Media and How It Matters*. Princeton, NJ: Princeton University Press, 2012. A Georgetown University government and public policy professor examines the weakening public trust in the US news media. He finds that this lack of confidence has changed how the public acquires political information and forms electoral preferences.

Periodicals and Internet Sources

Ayres, Carol Dark. "Is Media Bias Impairing Reporting on Benghazi?," *Kansas City (MO) Star*, May 23, 2014.

Barry, Colleen L., Marian Jarlenski, Rachel Grob, Mark Schlesinger, and Sarah E. Gollust. "News Media Framing of Childhood Obesity in the United States from 2000 to 2009," *Pediatrics*, July 1, 2011.

Buss, Dale. "*N.Y. Times* Denial of Media Bias Fails to Make Its Argument," *Forbes*, October 3, 2012.

Corcoran, Michael. "Blaming the Victims: Media Bias Against Struggling Millennials," Truthout, November 20, 2013. www.truth-out .org.

Gentzkow, Matthew, and Jesse M. Shapiro. "What Drives Media Slant? Evidence from U.S. Daily Newspapers," *Econometrica*, January 2010.

Glynn, Carroll J., and Michael E. Huge. "How Pervasive Are Perceptions of Bias? Exploring Judgments of Media Bias in Financial News," *International Journal of Public Opinion Research*, February 17, 2014.

Groeling, Tim. "Media Bias by the Numbers: Challenges and Opportunities in the Empirical Study of Partisan News," *Annual Review of Political Science*, May 2013.

Huston, Warner Todd. "The Top 50 Liberal Media Bias Examples," Western Journalism, December 10, 2011. www.westernjournalism.com.

Kiener, Robert. "Media Bias: Is Slanted Reporting Replacing Objectivity?," *CQ Researcher*, vol. 23, no. 17, 2013.

Lee, Eun-Ju. "That's Not the Way It Is: How User-Generated Comments on the News Affect Perceived Media Bias," *Journal of Computer-Mediated Communication*, October 2012.

McKeever, Brooke Weberling, Daniel Riffe, and Francesca Dillman Carpentier. "Perceived Hostile Media Bias, Presumed Media Influence, and Opinions About Immigrants and Immigration," *Southern Communication Journal*, November–December 2012.

Nuccitelli, Dana. "Conservative Media Outlets Found Guilty of Biased Global Warming Coverage," *The Guardian* (Manchester, UK), October 11, 2013.

Reagan, Michael. "Biased Media Celebrate Obamacare," Newsmax, April 3, 2014. www.newsmax.com.

Reynolds, Glenn Harlan. "Breaking Media Silence," *USA Today*, April 15, 2013.

Shafer, Jack. "Media Bias? Give Me More, Please!," Reuters, September 20, 2011. www.reuters.com.

Zummo, Paul. "Is Media Bias an Even Bigger Problem Now?," *American Catholic*, November 8, 2012.

Websites

Chicago Monitor (http://chicagomonitor.com). The *Chicago Monitor* is an online news publication that provides in-depth analysis of mainstream news and highlights unreported stories. Its website examines local, national, and international media coverage and also offers alternative perspectives to articles that demonstrate bias or sensationalism.

Columbia Journalism Review (www.cjr.org). The *Columbia Journalism Review* (CJR) was founded in 1961 with a mission to encourage excellence in journalism. CJR monitors and supports the press, and its website features resources for journalists, news articles about the industry, and commentary.

Editor & Publisher (www.editorandpublisher.com). *Editor & Publisher* is a journal that covers all aspects of the newspaper industry, from the newsroom to business, advertising, circulation, and technology. Its website provides news articles, opinion pieces, as well as resources such as its annual newspaper data book.

Grade the News (www.gradethenews.org). Grade the News is a media research project based at San Jose State University's School of Journalism and Mass Communications and affiliated with Stanford University's graduate program in journalism. The project analyzes local media coverage in the San Francisco Bay Area and offers a periodic survey of thousands of print and broadcast stories. Its website features an online discussion forum, a printable news scorecard for visitors to use at home, local media contacts, and resources about the journalism industry's code of ethics.

Tyndall Report (http://tyndallreport.com). The *Tyndall Report* monitors the weekday nightly newscasts of *ABC World News Tonight, CBS Evening News*, and *NBC Nightly News*. Its website offers commentary on each night's newscasts and links to the stories that were aired. In addition to the nightly monitoring, the website provides yearly reviews as well.

Index

Picture Credits

© Abdullah Doma/AFP/Getty Images, 70
© Andrew Harrer/Bloomberg via Getty Images, 46
© Brendan Smialowski/EdStock/iStock, 56
© Chris Batson/Alamy, 104
© Craig M. Eisenberg/Alamy, 14
© D Dipasupil/Getty Images, 83
© DOD Photo/Alamy, 128
© dotshock/Shutterstock.com, 93
© iQoncept/Shutterstock.com, 10
© Jonathan Wiggs/The Boston Globe via Getty Images, 75
© Jonny White/Alamy, 96
© Justin Sullivan/Getty Images, 51
© Maksim Shmeljov/Shutterstock.com, 121
© NetPhotos/Alamy, 37
© Newsies Media/Alamy, 65, 113
© Richard Levine/Alamy, 42
© Robin Marchant/Getty Images, 88
© Wim Wiskerke/Alamy, 28
© withGod/Shutterstock.com, 17